The Complete Buttons Collection

Anita Mulvey

Illustrated by Emily Thomas

The Complete Buttons Collection

by Anita Mulvey

This book was first published in Great Britain in paperback during February 2024.

The moral right of Anita Mulvey is to be identified as the author of this work and has been asserted by her in accordance with the Copyright, Designs and Patents Act of 1988.

All rights are reserved, and no part of this book may be produced or utilized in any format, or by any means, electronic or mechanical, including photocopying, recording or by any information storage or retrieval system, without prior permission in writing from the publishers - Coast & Country/Ads2life.
ads2life@btinternet.com

All rights reserved.

Copyright © February 2024 Anita Mulvey

ISBN: 979-8879472714

Buttons is a cat, a little black and white cat. Look carefully at her picture - can you see why she is called Buttons?

Buttons is a Manx cat so she was born without a tail. She lives at number 9 in a quiet cul-de-sac on the Isle of Man. Her humans are called Jim and Diane.

Contents

1. Hello Buttons! 1
2. Buttons in Trouble! 19
3. Buttons on Holiday 35
4. Christmas Buttons 51
5. Buttons Has a Plan 69
6. Easter Buttons 81
7. Buttons and the TT 97
8. Buttons in Love! 109
9. Buttons Visits the Vet 123
10. Buttons Saves the Day 135
11. Mollie's Manx Tails (the Buttons prequel) 149
Quizzes 175

Hello Buttons!

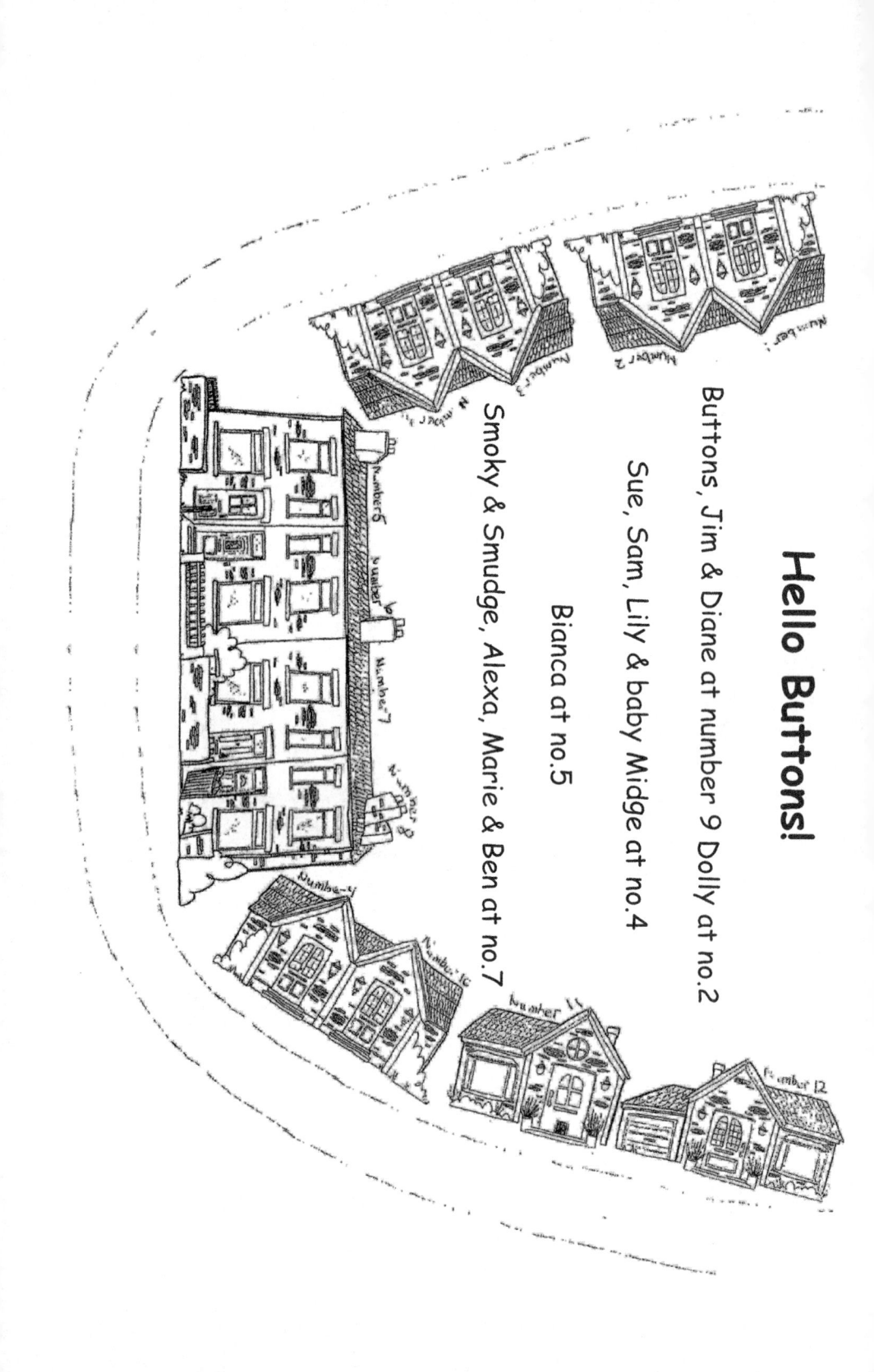

Hello Buttons!

Buttons, Jim & Diane at number 9 Dolly at no.2

Sue, Sam, Lily & baby Midge at no.4

Bianca at no.5

Smoky & Smudge, Alexa, Marie & Ben at no.7

Chapter 1

Buttons was asleep. Fast asleep.

As she lay curled up on the red cushion in her chair, the little Manx cat looked completely black. You might not even have noticed that she had been born without a tail. Her white chin was tucked between her black legs. Her white chest, tummy and even her white paws were out of sight. It wasn't until she turned over and stretched out in her sleep that the black spot of fur on her right front paw could be seen. Diane had laughed and called it a 'button' when she had first seen her tiny kitten. Months had passed since that day but the name had stuck. Everyone agreed that it was the perfect name for her, so 'Buttons' it was.

Suddenly Buttons heard a noise - half sigh, half yawn. Instantly Buttons was awake and absolutely starving. In fact, she was so hungry that she could hardly wait a moment more for her breakfast. She leaped from the comfort of her chair and landed expertly on Jim's chest. Immediately, Buttons began to press her front paws into Jim's body and chin.

Poor Jim! He pushed Buttons gently away from his face, muttering "Ok, ok, I'm getting up. Let's go then."

Buttons jumped onto the floor and waited impatiently while Jim pulled on his dressing gown. Jim put his hand on the door handle and Buttons was very pleased with his progress: maybe today all her past training efforts would pay off and he would go straight downstairs to get her breakfast. Alas, no! Jim went into the bathroom and locked the door.

Buttons scratched at the door, trying to get Jim's attention back on track. When he came out and started going down the stairs, Buttons weaved her body between his feet. Poor Jim had to stop every few steps or he would have fallen over her.

"We'd go much faster and safer if you didn't do that!" Jim moaned, but Buttons didn't understand. She was simply reminding Jim that she was there and needed feeding as soon as possible.

For Buttons and all the other cats in the neighbourhood, Operation Breakfast was the most important part of the morning. Buttons ran ahead of Jim into the kitchen. She sat next to her cupboard and pawed it to show Jim where her food was kept. Sadly, Jim could never remember and he leaned over her to fill up the kettle.

Buttons miaowed loudly and at last Jim bent down to fill up her food dish. Buttons was so hungry by now that she began eating even as Jim was putting her bowl on the floor. Buttons hoped that Operation Breakfast would go better tomorrow!

When she had eaten her fill, Buttons made her way to the back door and her cat flap. She looked out carefully – cats can never be *too* careful – and only went outside when she was certain that there was no danger for her there.

Once outside, Buttons began her Pussycat Patrol. This meant the very serious business of inspecting her back garden (it was definitely *her* garden, not Jim and Diane's, in Buttons' opinion anyway). Only when she was sure that no enemies had invaded her territory, did Buttons then move her Pussycat Patrol to her front garden and the rest of the cul-de-sac where she lived.

All was well, so Buttons went back indoors. She strolled through the house and paused by the dining table. Jim's new fleecy jacket was hanging over one of the chairs. Buttons sniffed the fleece, then gave it a little pat with her left front paw. She liked the feeling of the fleece on her claws. Buttons balanced carefully and reached up with both front paws so that she could have a lovely scratch on the fleece.

Suddenly, the jacket fell down on top of her. Terrified, Buttons escaped and ran for the safety of the windowsill. When she knew that the fleece had not followed her, she turned her back on it and pretended that she hadn't been frightened at all.

Now Buttons began her third job of the day: Big Wash. Like all cats, she took this job very seriously and put much care and attention into keeping her fur in perfect condition. In fact, she was so busy that she didn't even notice Jim moaning about finding his new jacket on the floor. Luckily, Jim didn't see the snags on the back of his fleece.

After a really good Big Wash, Buttons looked out of the window. From her seat on the sill, she could see which other cats in her cul-de-sac had been fed and were out on their Pussycat Patrols. The beautiful white cat Bianca, who lived in house number 5, was strolling along the road looking for danger as she went. The grey brothers Smoky and Smudge from number 7 were doing a great job of keeping their front lawn clear of sparrows.

Of Dolly, the little cat from number 2, there was no sign. She was a fellow Manx cat, but her fur had a beautiful tortoiseshell pattern instead of Buttons' black and white. Buttons knew that Dolly also had trouble keeping her humans on track with Operation Breakfast.

Since moving into the cul-de-sac two weeks ago, Buttons was determined to solve *all* the mysteries of her new neighbourhood. She still had lots of puzzles to solve, but her first one had been a great success. She now knew all the other cats and had found out where they lived. She had even gone into house number 7 when the grey brothers had not been looking. Unfortunately the human girl Alexa had seen Buttons, so her parents had crossly chased her away. But as she escaped through their cat flap Buttons pretended that it had been her idea to leave anyway.

Buttons' humans Jim and Diane were now ready for work and they set off, saying goodbye and giving her a little stroke. Buttons was so tired after all her work so far that she jumped down from the window ledge, found a sunny spot on the carpet and settled down for a nice nap.

After a lovely little sleep, Buttons began her Guard Cat Duty. This could be done from a window sill in the house or from outside if she wanted. Today she chose to keep watch from the garden, so she lay down under the bush by her front door.

Suddenly Buttons heard noises coming from house number 4. Sue had her car doors open and was strapping baby Midge into his car seat. Buttons watched with interest. She saw Sue driving off with her children on most days, but Buttons had no idea where they went or why Sue came back a short while later with only baby Midge in the car. Maybe today Buttons could find out.

As Sue went back indoors to fetch her two older children, the little cat jumped into the back of the car. She hid on the floor and played a great game of Pat-a-Cake with the baby's swinging feet. Sue didn't notice her at all. Having safely strapped Sam and Lily in their booster seats, Sue started up the car's engine and drove out of the cul-de-sac. Would Buttons solve this mystery today?

Chapter 2

While Sue was helping Sam and Lily out of the car, Buttons jumped onto the pavement. Curiously, she looked all around her but she didn't know where she was. It was a very busy place with people saying goodbye, parents checking that their children had their PE kits and lunch money, and children saying hello to their friends. Buttons was determined to find out what this mysterious place was so she slinked through the iron gates and made her way to the large brick building. Everyone was so busy that no-one saw Buttons slipping into the school.

Once inside the front doors, Buttons trotted into the cloakroom with the children. Again it was very busy. The children set about hanging up their bags and coats, while chatting about their weekends. For Buttons it was all rather noisy, so she went along the corridor where she found a room full of books and comfy chairs.

It was peaceful here, so she curled up on a cushion for a snooze. As she fell asleep, beautiful singing floated towards her from the hall where the children were in Assembly. What a lovely lullaby!

Some time later, a group of children arrived to read and were amazed to find the little cat. They stroked her and Buttons enjoyed the fuss they made of her. Just then they all heard the teacher's heels tapping on the wooden floor as she made her way into the library to lead her guided reading group. Buttons jumped down and hid behind the nearest bookcase.

The teacher, Miss Evans, didn't see her and the children had fun peeping at Buttons and trying not to giggle as they took turns to read. Buttons enjoyed listening to the story but she slinked out of the library when the children had finished reading and were writing about their favourite characters.

Next Buttons went into the hall and leapt up onto a sunny windowsill for a little rest. She hardly had time to sleep before a class arrived for their PE lesson. Some of the children spotted her, and called out in amazement.

"What is all this noise?" asked the teacher, Mr Carlton.

Most of the children were happy to see Buttons, but poor Tansy was scared of her. Her hands were shaking and she backed away as some of the others pointed at the window ledge.

"There's a cat in our school!" the children cried, but Buttons quickly jumped down and ran away before Mr Carlton could see her too.

Buttons ran into the nearest classroom. Here she found the children hard at work on their numeracy lesson. One group was working out the money in a role-play shop. The plastic coins interested Buttons and she tried to join in. The children laughed as she swiped a paw through the money, scattering coins over the carpet. The teacher came over then.

"What is going on here?" asked Mrs Bennett, "and what happened to those coins?"

"The cat knocked them over," the children explained, but Buttons was hiding under a table. Before Mrs Bennett could find her, Buttons had vanished.

In the next classroom, the children were doing art. Unfortunately, Buttons had never been in an art lesson before and she knocked over a water pot when she leapt onto the nearest table to find out what the class was doing. She was frightened by the excited cries of the children and ran over one of the paintings as she made her escape.

"This is much too noisy!" exclaimed the teacher, Miss Harris. "Oh dear," she added when she saw the puddle of water. "Go and fetch a cloth, Johnny," she said.

"The black and white cat did it!" explained the children, but of course Buttons had gone.

"Are you sure?" asked Miss Harris. "I've never seen a cat in school!"

"Yes," replied Joe, "and I can prove it!" he said. He held up his painting where Buttons had left a trail of purple paint paw prints right across his work. Luckily, Joe had a pet cat at home and he saw the funny side of the accident.

"It was a Manx cat," Justine said, but this puzzled some of the other children. "Manx cats don't have tails," she explained.

Miss Harris looked for the little cat, but Buttons had disappeared.

"Why don't Manx cats have tails?" Edward asked.

"Well," said Miss Harris, "do you remember Noah and his ark?"

As the children nodded, she continued, "Noah collected two of every animal and put them safely on the ark. He called the Manx cats to join him but they didn't come. When the rains started, Noah had to shut the door. The Manx cats jumped aboard just in time, but their tails got trapped by the door and were left behind. Of course, that's just a story. The truth is that Manx cats are born without tails; it's the way they are made."

The class were interested in the ark story but most of them were relieved to hear that it wasn't exactly true!

It was now playtime, so children all around the school tidied up and put on their coats to go out into the playground. The teachers who were not on playtime duty went to the staff room for a cup of tea.

"My guided group read very well today, but they were very giggly," Miss Evans told the other teachers.

"That sounds like my class at the start of our PE lesson," stated Mr Carlton.

"And my class seemed to find numeracy very funny today," added Mrs Bennett. "The children told me that there was a cat in the classroom, but I couldn't see it."

At that moment, Miss Harris came into the staff room for her cuppa. "Just look at this!" she said, holding up Joe's painting for all the staff to see. "We have a black and white visitor in our school today and here is the evidence to prove it!"

Everyone was surprised to see the painting with the paw prints on it.

"So, there *is* a cat in school today!" said Mrs Bennett. "Let's all look for it after break," she suggested.

And so, they did. All the children and staff searched for her but Buttons was nowhere to be found. Mr Gale, the head teacher, went back to his office. He pulled out his chair and there she was!

"I recognise you!" exclaimed Mr Gale. "You live in the cul-de-sac near my house. I'll take you back there but you will have to wait till lunch time. You have disrupted our school enough for one day and we've all got work to do now!"

So, Buttons spent the rest of the morning in the head teacher's office. But Mr Gale wanted his chair back. He found a box of paper and emptied it out. After putting a cushion in the box, he lifted Buttons up and put her in too. Buttons didn't mind. Mr Gale's cushion was very comfortable and she was very tired. She curled up and had a lovely long snooze.

Chapter 3

When Mr Gale had kindly taken her back to her cul-de-sac, Buttons trotted to her house and sat on the doorstep. She was feeling very pleased with herself. Today's investigation was a great success. She had found out where Sue's two oldest children went on most days and she had seen some of the things they did there. Buttons had lots of other mysteries to solve, but they could wait for now. She decided that school was fun but tiring. Maybe she would go there again one day, but not tomorrow.

After such a busy morning, Buttons needed a rest. She curled up under the bush next to her front door and fell asleep. Like all cats, however, she kept half an ear open so she could still be On Guard even when sleeping. This allowed her to wake up the moment a pigeon landed on her lawn. Buttons was immediately awake but she only needed to raise her head for the bird to notice her and fly away. Buttons was a very good Guard Cat.

The afternoon passed with Buttons taking much needed snoozes in between being aware of all the comings and goings of the animals and humans in her neighbourhood.

She was having a little nap when she heard the sound of Diane's car. Now Buttons must begin Diane's Teatime Training. As Diane opened the front door, Buttons rubbed her body on Diane's legs, twisting between them as Diane tried to unlace her boots and put on her slippers without falling over the little cat.

Buttons nearly started playing with the wriggly laces, but her tummy was rumbling. She bounded into the living room, mewing loudly to help with Diane's learning. Diane did very well and went straight to the cupboard where the cat food was kept. Buttons was very happy with Diane when she took out two little pouches of food.

"What would you like today – duck or fish?" she asked her pet.

Buttons nudged the fish pouch with her face and miaowed gladly as Diane threw away her leftover breakfast and cleaned her bowl. Then Buttons sat ready as Diane tipped the food into her dish and put it on the floor. Buttons didn't thank Diane – cats don't understand human manners. Instead she began eating her food, satisfied with her progress. Diane's Teatime Training was going very well.

When Buttons had eaten enough (saving the rest for later in case nothing better came her way), she padded to her cat flap and looked out. Satisfied that all was well, she went through the flap and had a little stroll around her garden. Then Buttons went and sat by her front door. Jim and Diane had placed a cat scratching post there for her, but Buttons ignored it and had a good scratch on the front door mat. Lovely! Feeling tired after so much effort, Buttons curled up on the doorstep and fell asleep.

After a while she heard Jim's car coming into the cul-de-sac. Buttons had a long stretch then rubbed her body on Jim's legs as he put his key into the door. Jim had to be very careful to open the door and walk into the house without tripping up, as Buttons was twisting between his legs and miaowing loudly.

"Alright then, girl, give me chance to hang up my coat," Jim said, but Buttons wasn't listening. She ran to the kitchen and sat by her cupboard. Jim followed her and opened the cupboard door. He chose a rabbit flavour food pouch, scraped the leftover food into the bin and put the new food in her dish. Buttons had just started eating when Diane came downstairs after changing out of her work clothes.

"Oh Jim, I've already given Buttons her tea!" Diane cried when she saw Jim with the empty food pouch.

Jim groaned. "Naughty cat," he said crossly, but Buttons didn't mind. This teatime was a triumph!

The evening passed with Buttons doing a late Pussycat Patrol followed by a long nap next to the tree in her front garden. She woke suddenly when it began to rain. She ran to the back door, rushed through the cat flap and bounded into the living room where she jumped onto Diane's lap.

"Ugh!" Diane moaned. "You're all wet!"

"Soggy moggy!" laughed Jim.

But Buttons didn't mind. Diane's lap was comfy and she was soon drying off with the warmth from Diane's legs. Buttons settled her chin comfortably on her paws and drifted off to sleep.

What a **wonderful** day.

Buttons In Trouble!

Buttons in Trouble!

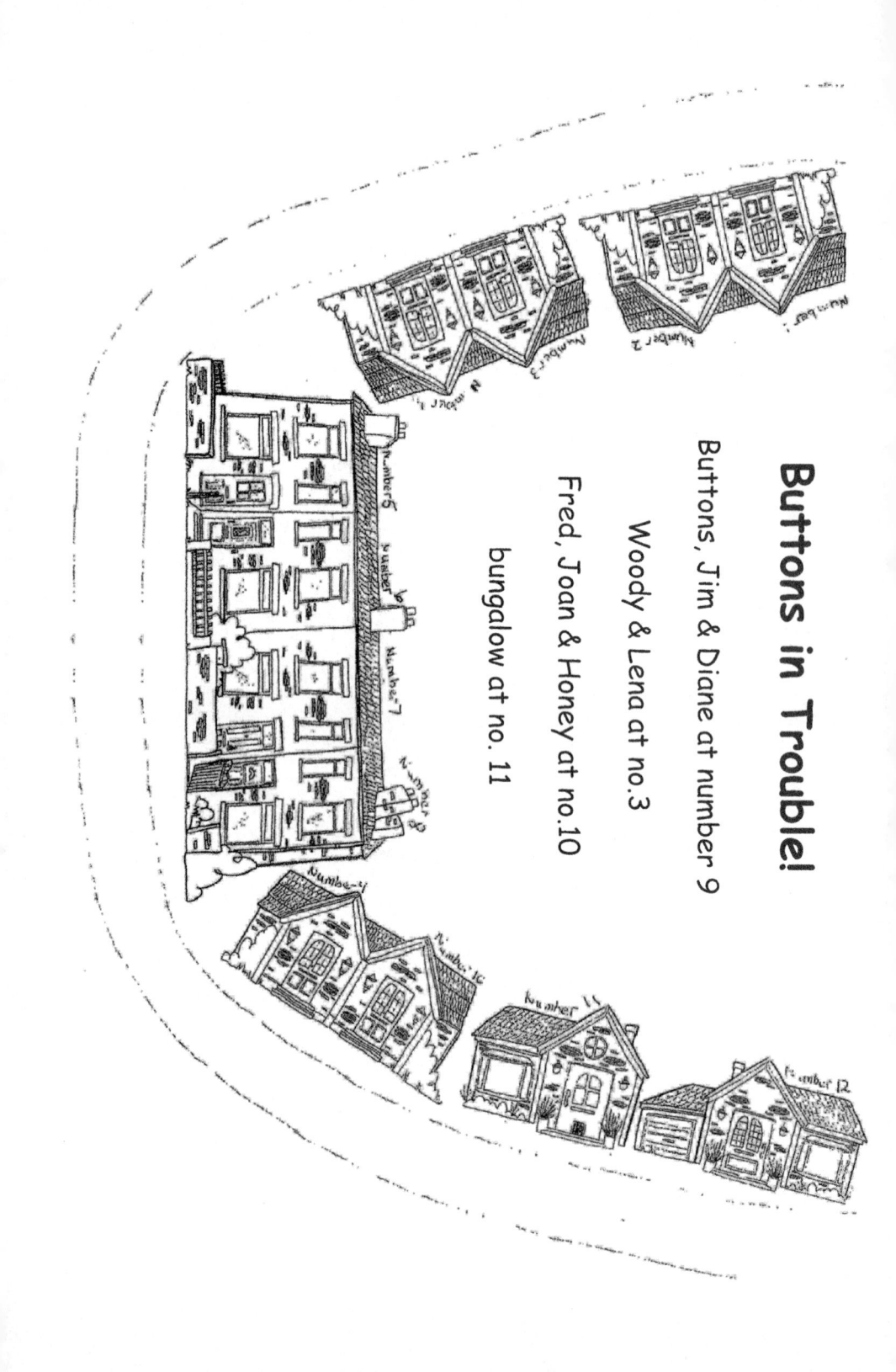

Buttons, Jim & Diane at number 9

Woody & Lena at no.3

Fred, Joan & Honey at no.10

bungalow at no. 11

Chapter 1

It was Saturday morning, a rather dull day in October. As usual, Buttons was awake and instantly starving when Jim got up and went into the bathroom. She miaowed unhappily and scratched at the bathroom door, but she didn't need to worry.

"Come on, Buttons, I'll get your breakfast today," said Diane, getting out of bed and going downstairs. "After all, it is your special day," she added.

Buttons didn't know what Diane meant by this, but she didn't fret about it as she tucked into her breakfast.

A short while later Diane picked up her car keys and said, "Now you be good today and stay out of trouble. Keep a look out for Granny who should be here around teatime. Granny is coming to stay with us for a few days and we'll all have a treat later as it's your special day."

Again, Buttons didn't understand what her special day might be. However, she recognised the word 'Granny' and knew that lots of tasty treats would be coming her way.

As Buttons went outside for her Pussycat Patrol, she considered the mysteries she still had to solve. She had only been living here for a few weeks but she had already solved some puzzles. She had met all the cats and dogs and knew where they lived. She had also met most of the humans in the road and found out where some of them went when they left the cul-de-sac.

Buttons made her way into the garden of the house next door. She had no idea why the grass was so long here – Jim called it a jungle! She climbed onto a window ledge and looked in. Why had she never seen anyone there? And now Diane had given her another puzzle: what was her 'special day'?

The little Manx cat walked right around the neighbourhood. She saw no danger anywhere so she went home. Buttons did her Big Wash before settling down for a nice nap on Diane and Jim's bed.

Suddenly she heard a strange noise coming from her back garden.

It was a sort of swishing noise. She had to investigate!

Buttons jumped down and quickly ran down the stairs. She rushed to her cat flap and looked out, but couldn't see what was making the odd noise. Feeling very brave, she pushed through the flap to go outside and find out.

Buttons was amazed to discover that Jim was responsible. He had a broom and was sweeping up all the leaves which had fallen from the trees. Buttons thought this was a marvellous game and she ran up and down the path, getting in the way of Jim's broom and scattering the leaves as he tried to brush them into a pile.

Jim and Buttons had a great game for a few minutes, but Jim soon tired of it as he wanted to get the garden tidy.

"Ok, Buttons," said Jim, "please go and play somewhere else."

But Buttons didn't understand. She jumped in front of the broom again and nearly got swept up with the leaves.

"Enough, Buttons," Jim said impatiently.

But still Buttons didn't stop. She ran through the leaves, making them swirl through the air.

"Now you're being very naughty!" Jim cried crossly.

Poor Buttons. She didn't like being told off and turned her back on Jim, pretending that it was her idea to stop the game. Unfortunately, she was still in the way so Jim picked her up and took her to the front of the house. He put her down on the door step.

"Now stay here and keep out of trouble!" said Jim.

Buttons was not happy but just then she was distracted as a large van came around the corner and pulled up right in front of the house next door. She watched with interest as a man and woman got out and opened the back of the van.

These strange humans unlocked the front door of house number 10. Together they took a large box out of the van and carried it indoors.

Buttons was intrigued and watched as the strangers carried more things from the van into the house. Then a little sandy coloured dog appeared and began barking furiously.

Jim came back to the front garden to see where the barking was coming from. He met the two new humans who were also wondering what their dog was barking at.

"Quiet, Honey!" the man ordered. Then he turned to Jim and said, "Hello. My name is Fred and this is my wife Joan. This noisy puppy is Honey."

"Hello. I'm Jim," stated Jim. "Are you moving in here?" he asked, pointing to the house next door.

"Yes," Fred said. He looked at Honey who was still barking. She was also straining against his hand on her collar and trying to get into the back of the van.

"Stop it," he cried. "What is the matter with you?"

"Welcome to our neighbourhood," said Jim kindly. "I will introduce you to my wife Diane when she comes home later. We have a Manx cat called Buttons."

Jim stopped then and looked all around. Little Buttons was nowhere to be seen.

"I think I might know why Honey is barking," Jim told his new neighbours. He pointed at the van and they all walked over to look inside.

And there was Buttons, curled up cosily on Fred and Joan's sofa!

It was chaos then. Jim told Buttons to get out; Fred and Joan were laughing; Honey barked even louder and Buttons pretended that she always had nice naps on sofas in the back of vans.

Buttons, like all cats, doesn't take much notice when told what to do, but she decided that she wanted to get out of the van anyway. She jumped down onto the pavement and paused by the puppy. For a few seconds, Jim held his breath while the cat and dog just looked at each other.

Honey sniffed Buttons and then the two young animals agreed to be good friends. After that they had a marvellous game of chase on the front gardens. The humans laughed as the animals took turns to be the chaser.

"Well, we must get back to unloading the van," said Joan.

She called to Honey, then Fred and Joan carried another box into their new house.

Buttons sat on her doorstep feeling very pleased with herself. Another mystery solved - hooray! She lay down for a much-needed rest after all her running with Honey.

Chapter 2

Jim went indoors to have a cup of tea before fetching some bin bags to collect up the pile of leaves. He had only just sat down with his cuppa when he heard more barking. He looked out of the window to see that this time it was the Dalmatian dog from house number 3. This dog was called Woody and he was barking excitedly and running after a little ball being thrown for him by his owner, Lena.

As Jim watched, Woody ran along the cul-de-sac with the ball in his mouth. Suddenly Woody dropped the ball and started to chase something, something which Jim couldn't see. Then a lot of noise came from the back garden.

"Oh, no!" thought Jim as he put his mug down and ran to the back window. He was just in time to see Buttons being chased by Woody. Buttons jumped right into the pile of leaves, spreading them everywhere.

Jim groaned, but he couldn't help smiling as the two animals leaped happily through all the flying leaves. Woody and Buttons were good friends and they had a fantastic game together.

When Jim went outside, he found that Woody had gone. Buttons, however, was still there surrounded by leaves.

"Naughty cat," sighed Jim. "No more playing with these leaves!"

Buttons set about giving her fur a quick wash while Jim sadly swept up the leaves *again*. Jim was very busy and placed the first full bin bag in the dustbin. He was just on the point of putting in the second bag when he heard a sad miaow. He stopped and looked all around, but couldn't see Buttons anywhere. He shrugged then leaned over the dustbin. There was another miaow, even louder this time. He looked inside the bin. To his surprise, he could see a pair of cat eyes looking back at him from inside the dustbin!

When Diane returned shortly afterwards, she found Jim next to the upside-down dustbin, surrounded by bin bags and leaves.

"What on Earth are you doing?" she asked in amazement.

"Buttons fell inside the bin!" Jim explained. "She is now on the sofa having another Big Wash. I hope that she can stay out of any more trouble!"

Diane shook her head then went indoors too. She made herself and Jim a nice cup of tea, taking Jim's outside for him. When she returned, she sat next to Buttons who was just finishing her second Big Wash of the day. What a Saturday morning! Buttons was exhausted. She climbed happily onto Diane's lap for a little snooze.

Chapter 3

Buttons had a much more peaceful afternoon. Diane went to the hairdressers, Jim washed his car and Buttons had a really long nap under the bush by her front door.

She woke up when the postman arrived with a parcel for the humans who lived in the bungalow at number 11. He dropped a red elastic band by their front door which Buttons had to investigate. She tried to play with it but soon gave up this game when the elastic pinged her paw.

Later Buttons was having a little snooze by the tree in her back garden when she heard a car drive into the road. Hooray – it was Granny in her little, red car!

Granny parked on the drive and opened her car door. Quick as a flash, Buttons ran to her and began to miaow, rubbing her body against Granny's legs.

"Here, this is for you," Granny told her, reaching into her pocket for a cat biscuit.

Buttons munched her treat and immediately mewled for more.

"No more for now," Granny said. "It's almost teatime and we don't want to spoil your appetite."

Buttons didn't care about spoilt appetites and miaowed again. Granny got her suitcase out of her car boot and placed it on the doorstep. She rang the doorbell but Jim was using the vacuum cleaner and didn't hear it.

"We'll just have to wait for a few minutes," said Granny.

Buttons thought that Granny's Teatime Training should begin now. To help Granny, Buttons scratched at the front door.

"I don't have a key. We won't have long to wait now," Granny told the impatient little cat. She rang the doorbell again but Jim still couldn't hear it.

But Buttons didn't understand what the problem was. She was hungry and needed her tea **now**. She wanted Granny's attention so she pawed at Granny's leg. Unfortunately, her claws got stuck in Granny's tights. Buttons pulled her paw away as Granny tried to untangle her claws. There was a ripping sound as the tights laddered right down to Granny's ankle!

"Naughty Buttons!" Granny exclaimed. "It's lucky that it's your special day or I would be really cross with you!"

Once again, Buttons wondered about her 'special day'. She planned to solve this mystery **soon**.

Just then, Jim finished vacuuming so he heard the bell at last and opened the door. Buttons left Granny and rubbed her body on his legs, purring happily. Jim's Teatime Training was much better than Granny's.

Because it was her special day, Jim chopped up a fresh tuna steak for Buttons' tea. Buttons was delighted and decided that she should have fresh fish **every** day from now on.

Jim prepared some new potatoes and vegetables for his tea with Diane and Granny, while Granny baked a chocolate birthday cake. Jim had just started to grill the rest of the tuna steaks when Diane arrived home with a present for Buttons.

"We'll open your present after tea," Diane told the little cat.

Jim got distracted by this and one of the steaks started to burn, setting off the smoke alarm. Jim turned the steaks over while Diane waved a tea towel under the smoke detector, but the noise didn't stop.

Granny decided that something bigger was needed to clear the air, so she grabbed the large box of cornflakes off the shelf and started waving it under the detector. This did work and the alarm stopped beeping. However, the lid of the box came open and cornflakes flew in a majestic arc across the kitchen!

Buttons had been hiding under the dining table to escape the frightening noise. As soon as it stopped, she ran into the kitchen and jumped joyfully into the cornflakes. Buttons loved her Granny!

After some emergency vacuuming, the humans finished cooking and enjoyed their meal. Then they sat in the living room with a cup of tea and a slice of birthday cake. Granny showed Buttons the cake which she'd made in honour of her birthday, but Buttons wasn't interested.

"Come here, Buttons," Granny said. "I've got something you *will* like."

She fetched a little packet from her handbag, opened it and poured some of the contents into the palm of her hand. Buttons was intrigued and came to investigate. She sniffed the treats Granny offered her, then gave them an experimental lick. Deciding that they were tasty, Buttons ate them up and miaowed for more.

"What are those?" Diane asked.

"Chocolate buttons made specially for cats," Granny explained. "I think she likes them," she added.

Buttons nudged the little packet with her face and Granny kindly gave her a few more.

"Buttons loves buttons," Jim laughed. Diane and Granny laughed too.

"Now we'll open your birthday present," said Diane.

She opened the box and took out a pink, fleecy, S-shaped thing. Buttons didn't know what it was, but Jim and Granny didn't know either.

"It's a Radiator Slouch Pouch," Diane told everyone.

She hooked one end over the radiator and then they could all see the other end sticking out horizontally.

"Buttons can sleep here and be warm and cosy," said Diane.

She picked Buttons up and placed her in the comfy Slouch Pouch, but Buttons was having none of it. She jumped right out and looked scornfully at her present. Diane tried again, but Buttons immediately jumped right out again. She turned her back on the Slouch Pouch to show her displeasure at it.

"Never mind," Jim said to Diane. "Buttons will get used to it and then she is bound to love it."

Diane smiled and switched on the television. They all settled down to watch a film. Granny was tired after a long day and she soon nodded off to sleep. Buttons was delighted: Granny was the perfect visitor, in her opinion! She jumped onto Granny's lap and turned around to get into the best position for a little snooze with Granny.

Buttons had enjoyed her mysterious special day even though she had been in trouble earlier. She thought that special days were very tiring. Buttons decided that she would like another birthday, but **not** tomorrow.

Buttons on Holiday!

Buttons on Holiday

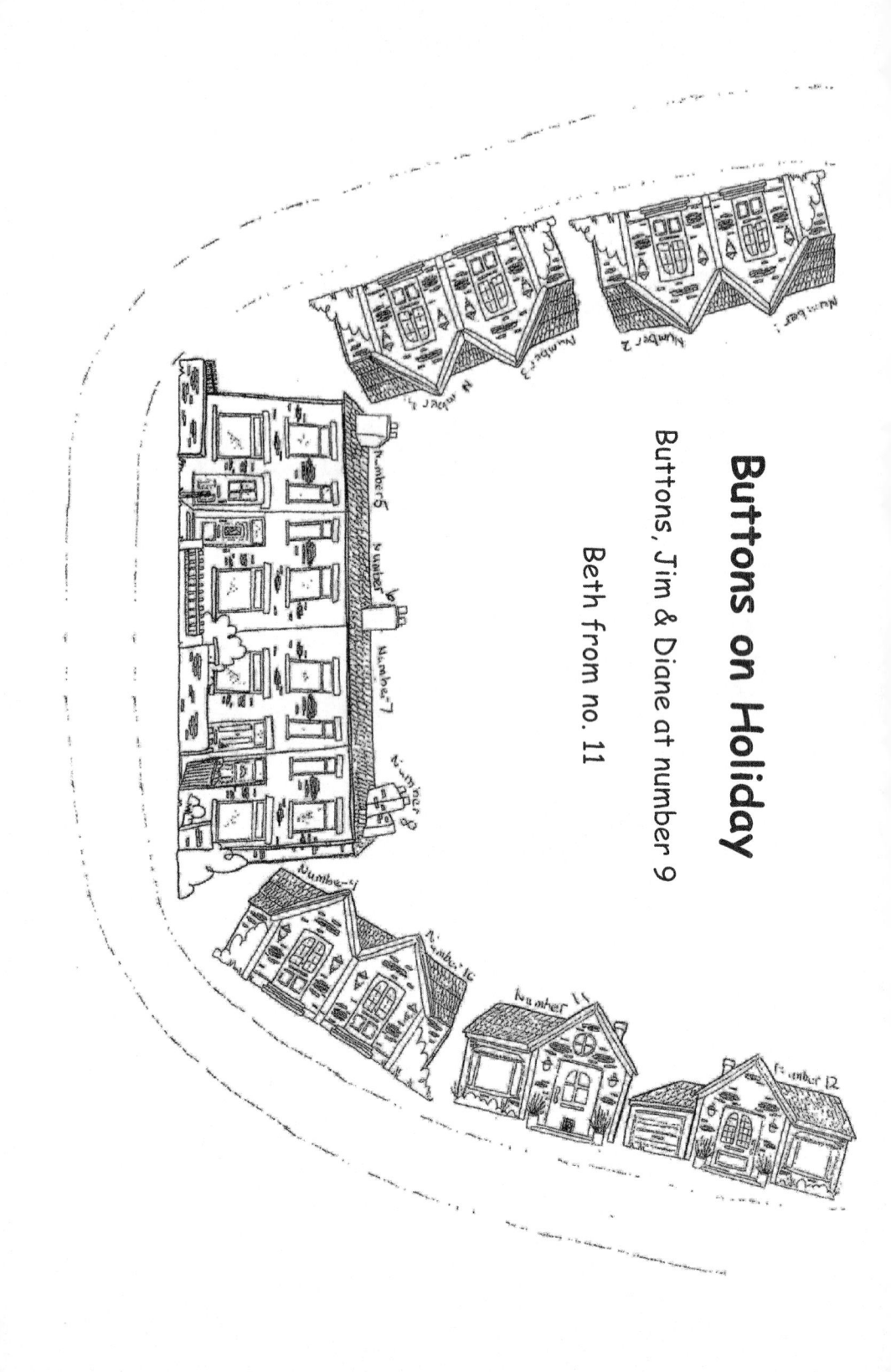

Buttons, Jim & Diane at number 9

Beth from no. 11

Chapter 1

Curled up on her chair in the bedroom, Buttons was happily snoozing. It was a sunny Summer Friday in July and she was having a lovely dream about mice.

However, she woke with a start when Jim pulled the suitcases down from the top of the wardrobe. Immediately, Buttons was suspicious.

Diane and Jim were excited because they were going on holiday the next day to Greece, but Buttons wasn't excited. She watched as her humans started packing their suitcases. Now she *knew* that something was going on and she wasn't at all happy about it.

Buttons went downstairs and found something even worse: her Cat Box had appeared in the living room! She did her best to ignore it and jumped up on the sunny window ledge for her Guard Cat Duty.

Packing finished, Jim and Diane came downstairs.

"Right, I'll hold the cat box and you can pick Buttons up and put her inside," Diane said to Jim.

But Buttons didn't agree with this plan. As Jim came nearer, she ran to her cat flap and escaped to the safety of the garden.

"I will tempt her back in with some fresh chicken," Diane said to Jim. "Get ready to catch Buttons when she is eating her snack."

Diane went into the back garden where Buttons was trying to hide in the flowerbed.

"Come on then, girl," Diane encouraged, holding out the treat for her.

As Buttons moved closer to Diane's outstretched hand and sniffed the chicken, Diane walked slowly backwards. The little Manx cat kept coming nearer to where Jim stood ready by the back door with the cat box at his feet. But Buttons was too fast for her humans. She dashed forward and took the offered treat from Diane and was climbing up the tree before they had any chance to catch her. Button sat safely out of reach and looked down sadly on her treacherous owners.

"Let's leave her for a bit," Jim suggested. "When she has had time to forget all about the cat box, we can try to tempt her again."

"Good idea," Diane agreed. "Thank goodness we have all morning to get her to my sister's house so Paula can look after Buttons while we are on holiday."

Jim and Diane went indoors. Jim opened a can of tuna and placed some in the cat's dish. He put the cat box on the table so it would be out of sight when Buttons came in.

Half an hour passed and Buttons did not come in, then an hour and still Buttons had not appeared.

"Right," said Jim. "I'll go outside with the bowl of tuna. I will let Buttons have a little taste and then she will be tempted to come in for more. You get ready to catch her this time."

Jim went outside and waved the cat bowl around the tree, trying to waft the scent of tuna up to Buttons. Buttons took no notice.

Then Jim fetched his ladder and put it against the tree. Diane held it at the bottom for safety while Jim climbed up. Buttons watched as Jim placed a spoonful of tuna on her branch. She was a clever cat and so she was suspicious – Jim didn't usually climb trees to feed her!

Jim went down a couple of rungs on the ladder and Buttons knew that she could now get the snack safely out of Jim's reach. She walked proudly along her branch and ate the tasty tuna. This was a triumph – hopefully Buttons could train Jim to feed her treats this way every day from now on.

Jim wafted the fishy smell around again and Buttons was tempted. She started climbing down the tree as Jim went down the ladder. In this way, they both got back on the ground. Jim put the dish on the grass. Diane was ready and she pounced on Buttons as the little cat took a mouthful of tuna.

"Quick, Jim, get the cat box," Diane cried as she struggled with the wriggling cat.

Jim did so and together the humans managed to get Buttons into her hated cat box.

"At last!" cried Jim with relief, locking the cat box so Buttons couldn't escape.

"That took us nearly two hours!" Diane exclaimed. "Let's drive over to Paula's house now. We'll take the dish with us and Buttons can eat the rest of the tuna when we get there."

Poor Buttons mewed sadly all the way to Paula's house. But she soon cheered up when she was let out of the box in Paula's living room. Buttons had already trained Aunty Paula last year and she knew that many snacks would be offered whenever she wanted. Buttons was happy; she was going to have a wonderful holiday with Aunty Paula.

Chapter 2

The next morning was a Saturday and Paula decided to do some gardening. Buttons loved to help and so she ran up and down Paula's pretty garden. Every now and again, Buttons jumped into the flowerbed where Paula was weeding. Then she played Pat-a-Cake with Paula's trowel as she worked. What fun!

After a little while Buttons tired of gardening. She curled up in a nice warm spot on the patio for a much-needed nap. However, she soon felt too hot so moved into the shade underneath Paula's deckchair.

Paula finished working on her flowerbeds. She was hot too so she went indoors and put on some sunscreen. She added some ice cubes to a glass of water and sat down to relax on her deckchair. She felt rather sleepy in the warmth of the day, and she closed her eyes for a little snooze. Buttons approved.

When Paula awoke, she reached down beside the deckchair for her drink, but her glass was empty.

Mystified, Paula looked around the garden and spotted Buttons. Buttons sat nearby enjoying the sunshine again. She was licking her whiskers, feeling very happy to be on holiday with Aunty Paula. Diane and Jim needed training to bring Buttons nice drinks when she wanted!

That evening, Paula prepared some vegetables and took a beef joint out of her freezer. She wanted the meat to defrost overnight so she could cook it for her friends who were coming for lunch the next day. She put the beef in a large dish on the worktop. When she went up to bed, Paula closed the kitchen door.

The next morning was Sunday, Paula's favourite day of the week and she was looking forward to cooking a special roast lunch for her friends. Paula showered and started to get herself ready for the day.

Suddenly she realised that something was wrong. No Buttons! Buttons wasn't there, pestering her for breakfast. Feeling rather worried, Paula hurried downstairs.

What a sight greeted her. Buttons was lying on her side on the sofa. Clearly, she wasn't well. Even worse, there was a nasty smell: Buttons had been sick on the carpet!

"Oh no!" exclaimed Paula. "Poor Buttons. Have you had fur balls to make you sick?"

Paula knew that cats are sometimes sick, because they get their own fur in their stomachs when they lick themselves clean. Paula went into her kitchen to fetch a cloth and her carpet cleaning spray.

Oh dear – what a mess she found in her kitchen! The metal dish was on the floor, upside down. The joint of beef was also on the floor and looked very ragged around the edges. Then Paula realised what had happened: during the night, Buttons had somehow managed to open the kitchen door and then climbed onto the worktop to eat some of the meat. Buttons must have knocked the dish onto the floor.

Paula looked in dismay at all the mess. She was cross with Buttons, but she couldn't feel *too* cross. She knew that cats have to follow their instincts and the smell of the beef must have been a great temptation. She picked up the meat, but it was past saving. Sadly she put it into the bin, then set about cleaning up the kitchen and the living room carpet. By the time she had finished, Buttons was looking a bit better and even managed to eat some breakfast.

Paula ate a slice of toast and jam while looking in her freezer. Unfortunately, she didn't have anything else which would make a special meal for her friends and she didn't have time to go shopping. How her friends laughed when they came to lunch: roast potatoes and vegetables with fish fingers. Most unusual but tasty anyway!

Buttons enjoyed a fish finger too, although she carefully spat out all the breadcrumb coating! It was great to be on holiday with Aunty Paula and Buttons knew that they would have a lovely week together.

Buttons had no way of knowing that she would have a mystery to solve before the week was out.

Chapter 3

Aunty Paula's doorbell rang and there were voices downstairs, but Buttons was too busy snoozing to go down and investigate.

The doorbell rang again and still Buttons was determined to sleep. She was so comfortable on Aunty Paula's bed!

However, when the pesky doorbell rang *again*, she sighed in her sleep. More voices floated up and disturbed her, and Buttons thought that Granny's voice was one of them. There was nothing for it; she just **had** to wake up and discover what was going on.

A strange sight met Buttons when she went downstairs. The doors between the living and dining rooms were wide open to make one big space. The coffee table had been moved into the kitchen and all the other furniture had been pushed back against the walls. But that wasn't the oddest thing. The really strange thing was that the room was full of people and they were all putting mats down on the floor!

Buttons had no idea what was going on, but she was determined to solve the mystery.

Buttons spotted Granny and joined her immediately. Granny stroked the little Manx cat then lay down on her mat. Buttons was amazed! Granny had never done this before, but Buttons was delighted anyway.

To her utter astonishment, everyone in the room started lying down on their mats as well, including Aunty Paula. Buttons was overjoyed to see lots of humans lying down. Cats spend most of their time relaxing and Buttons thought this was a huge improvement on the humans' more common sitting position. Joyfully she lay down next to Granny and wondered what would happen next.

One woman started telling the others how to breathe slowly and deeply. Buttons already knew how to breathe, so she didn't really listen.

As Marsha, the yoga teacher, told her class how to relax different parts of their bodies, Buttons crept over to Aunty Paula and jumped onto her tummy. Paula cried out in surprise and the teacher gently reminded everyone to be peaceful and quiet during relaxation. Poor Aunty Paula!

Buttons lay down on Paula's tummy and helped her to breathe and relax. Buttons was very good at breathing and relaxing.

As the class was taught how to stretch in different ways, Buttons slinked over to help Granny again. Unfortunately, Granny didn't see her coming and Buttons only just missed being accidentally kicked as Granny stretched out a leg.

"Naughty cat," Granny whispered and lifted Buttons off her mat and placed her safely on the sofa, but Buttons was far too interested in the yoga to stay there.

"Now we will move into the Mountain pose," said Marsha as she showed everyone how to get this tall balance.

Arthur, one of three men in the group, was quite new to yoga. He balanced on one leg and raised his arms slowly above his head. He was feeling very pleased with himself when Buttons rubbed her body around the ankle of his supporting leg. She tickled him with her fur and he wobbled badly. He almost managed to recover his balance before he stumbled forwards.

"More of an avalanche than a mountain!" his wife Carla whispered to him with a smile on her face.

"Great effort everybody," the teacher said. "We will now try the Bridge balance," she continued, showing her class how to get into this pose.

Buttons was intrigued as she watched the humans lie on their backs, bend their knees and place their feet flat on their mats. As they raised their bodies to make the sloping balance on their feet and shoulders, the little cat leaped effortlessly onto Carla's knees. She travelled down Carla's bridge as the poor woman tried hard to concentrate. However, as Buttons slowly crossed the bridge and came face to face with Carla, she shook and swayed and finally fell down, giggling.

"At least *my* bridge is not like London Bridge in that old song!" Arthur whispered to Carla, grinning.

Then the group moved on to the Warrior pose. Buttons admired the straight back leg of a woman dressed in green stretchy leggings and matching top. Her front leg was bent at the knee and made a perfect perch for Buttons to see what was going on. The poor lady was caught out and she struggled to keep her balance even though she had been practising yoga for years.

Marsha said, "Well done everyone. Let's do the Eagle pose now. You need to balance on one toe and twist your other leg around it..."

She got no further as her class started laughing.

"Oh dear," the teacher smiled too. "Buttons has quite put me off there. Let's start this posture by balancing on one **foot**!"

She went on to tell her class how to twist their legs round each other and do the same with their arms.

"If you are quite new to yoga, you can hold the balance there," Marsha continued, "but if you are more experienced you might like to bend your upper body forward like eagle wings."

Buttons had never seen a real eagle, but she had seen lots of garden birds and seagulls. As she looked around the room she thought that these people made the strangest looking birds that she had ever seen.

Then Buttons recognised Beth, from house number 11 in her cul-de-sac. Beth was doing her best to get the eagle balance right. However, she was very wobbly and her eagle was rocking rather wildly. She concentrated hard and might have managed to keep still if Buttons hadn't chosen that moment to pat her leg and miaow loudly, hoping for a little snack (Buttons had trained Beth to do this when she visited her bungalow). Poor Beth collapsed in a heap on her mat in a fit of giggles.

Next everybody was shown how to do the Boat balance. To do this, you need to sit down and hold your legs straight out and up, so that your body is in a triangular shape with your arms held out straight towards your feet. Buttons liked this pose and leaped onto Richard's middle. His boat hit choppy waters as he fought to keep his balance with a cat on his tummy.

"Enough, naughty Buttons!" said Aunty Paula, picking the little cat up and putting her out of the way in an armchair. "Now stay there and stop disturbing our yoga," she added.

After that, the class moved into the Puppy pose. Cats are actually very good at this position too, so Buttons could not resist jumping down and doing it perfectly alongside Eliza.

"Let's try the Face-Down Dog pose now," said the teacher, as she showed the pose for her class.

All the humans tried their best to follow her instructions, and Marsha went around the room helping people to make little changes to improve their posture. Geoff had his eyes shut so he could concentrate fully on getting in the correct position. He was doing very well and opened his eyes to find Buttons right in front of his face. She was very curious about this posture, but Geoff was totally distracted as her whiskers went right up his nose! He swayed wildly to and fro but could not get the balance again. He crumpled onto his mat where he lay for a few minutes trying not to feel cross with Buttons.

"I'm so sorry everybody," Paula said. "Buttons is being such a nuisance. Luckily, she is going home tomorrow and will not be here next week!"

Then Marsha had a brilliant idea.

"Let's finish up our balancing today with the Cat pose," she said.

Marsha told everyone to get on their hands and knees (just like having four paws, Buttons thought). Then Marsha showed her class how to arch their backs and look down through their arms at their knees. Just at that moment, Buttons strolled onto Marsha's mat and had a good stretch, showing this pose perfectly. Clever Buttons!

"You see what wonderfully flexible spines cats have," said Marsha. "Now we need to reverse this pose," she continued, showing the movement to the group.

"Right, everybody, time for our finishing relaxation," Marsha said.

As the curious cat watched, the humans lay down on their mats again. Some of them covered themselves with little blankets and Buttons approved of getting cosy. She joined Granny once more and snuggled up with her while Marsha read a peaceful poem and played some soothing music to finish the class. Buttons decided that she was definitely a fan of this strange thing called yoga.

As the humans began rolling up their mats and saying goodbye, Buttons vanished upstairs. She felt happy because she had successfully solved the mysteries of yoga, but was now quite worn out. She jumped onto Aunty Paula's bed for a much-needed nap.

Buttons thought that this morning had been a wonderful way to end her holiday with Aunty Paula but she wasn't sure that she could manage yoga **every** week!

Christmas Buttons

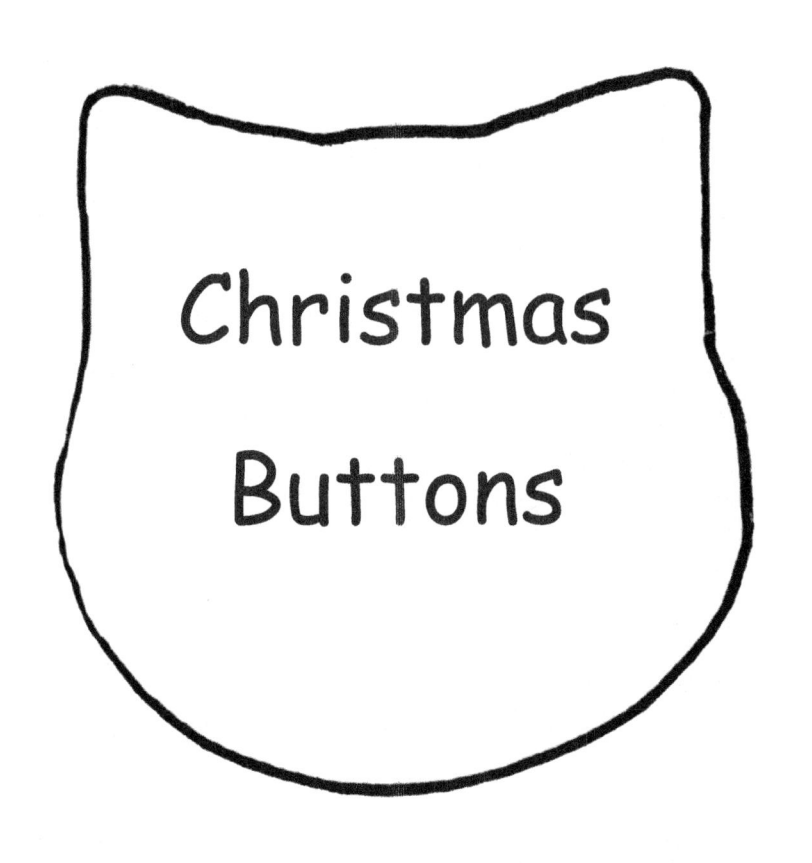

Christmas Buttons

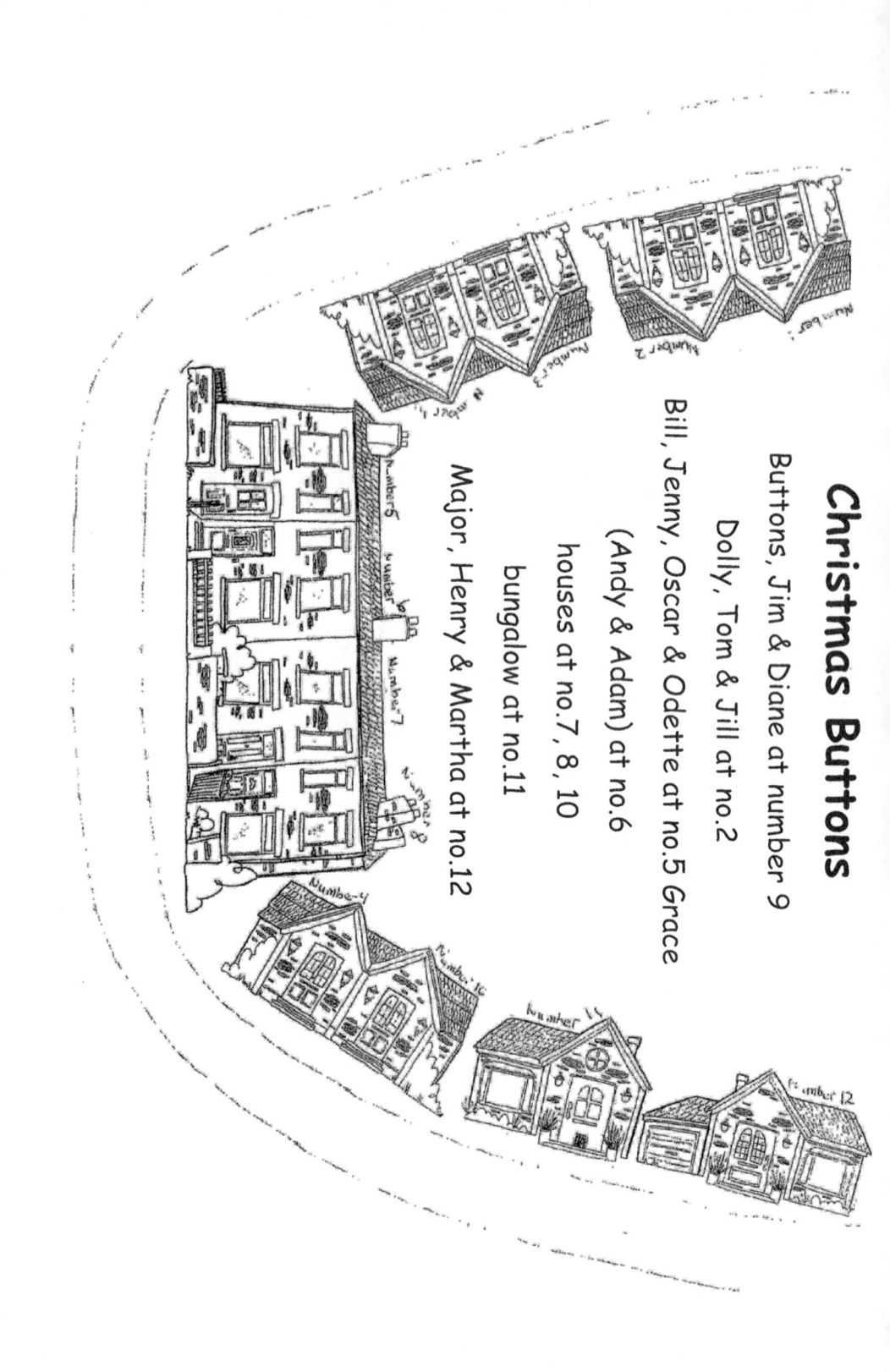

Buttons, Jim & Diane at number 9

Dolly, Tom & Jill at no.2

Bill, Jenny, Oscar & Odette at no.5 Grace (Andy & Adam) at no.6

houses at no.7, 8, 10

bungalow at no.11

Major, Henry & Martha at no.12

Chapter 1

Buttons, like all cats, was a curious creature. She loved exploring and particularly enjoyed solving mysteries. Sometimes she chose a puzzle to investigate and sometimes she found herself in the middle of a puzzle. Today was one of those days and she just had to find out what was going on all around her.

Hearing joyful cries outside, Buttons had a long stretch and a little scratch on the back door mat before going outside for her morning Pussycat Patrol.

First of all, Buttons noticed that pretty trees were appearing in most of the homes in her cul-de-sac. Even more strange, people were decorating these new trees with coloured lights, tinsel and sparkly baubles. Some houses even had twinkly lights and decorations in their front gardens. Buttons was amazed.

Still wondering what was going on, Buttons finished her Patrol and returned home. There she found Jim and Diane fetching a large box from the loft. Immediately she began to investigate and jumped up to peer inside the box.

"Get down, please, Buttons," said Jim, smiling at the curious little cat.

Buttons watched, fascinated, as Jim pulled a tree out of the box and started arranging its branches. Diane took some beautiful baubles out of the box and began putting them on the tree while Jim strung loops of coloured lights around it.

Buttons wanted to help, so she swiped a paw at a red bauble hanging on one of the lowest branches. The bauble fell off the tree and bounced away from her. Buttons chased after it, catching it then pushing it away again to repeat this fun game. Diane and Jim laughed, but Diane took the bauble away from Buttons.

"It's not a toy ball. It is delicate and might break," Diane said. "Maybe Father Christmas will bring you some toys to play with," she added.

Buttons didn't understand that, but she was distracted by the tinsel which Jim was taking out of the box. Delighted with this new game, Buttons caught hold of one end of a long string of red tinsel. She pulled hard with her teeth and claws as Jim tried to wrap his end around the tree. Buttons and Jim had a little game of Tug-of-War with the tinsel, until Jim realised that Buttons had hold of the other end.

"Diane," he said to his wife, "we'll have to put everything higher up the tree this year, out of Buttons' reach."

And so, they did. They added more decorations to the house: tinsel was wound round the bannister rail and draped over the mantelpiece; a snowman ornament was placed on the window sill; a red ribbon was strung around the chimney breast with Christmas cards on it and a Santa Claus ornament took pride of place in the middle of the mantelpiece. Finally, they hung some sparkly snowflakes from the ceiling. All of this was new to Buttons and she took some time to watch her busy humans before she curled up on the sofa for a much-needed snooze.

Jim and Diane went out to do their Christmas shopping and so Buttons was alone when she woke up. She gazed in wonder at the Christmas tree. It looked beautiful and Buttons needed to investigate this strange tree which had come out of a box. She jumped onto the highest branch that she could reach and started to scramble up even further. Unfortunately, the tree wasn't designed for cats to climb. As she tried to get higher, the tree wobbled and began to sway with Buttons gripping on to its plastic trunk.

The tree lurched from side to side and almost righted itself, but not quite. Suddenly it fell over completely with a crash. Buttons leaped to the safety of the window ledge. She sat and looked sadly at the odd tree which was now lying on its side, surrounded by sparkles and twinkles.

When Jim and Diane came home, they had a nasty shock when they saw all the mess.

"Naughty Buttons!" Jim cried, but the little Manx cat was nowhere to be seen.

That evening, after Buttons had a successful Teatime Training with Jim giving her some lovely fresh chicken to eat, Buttons found herself alone again. Diane and Jim were out carol singing. Buttons didn't know what this was, nor did she understand what her humans meant when they told her to keep out of trouble.

After a nice nap on the rug in front of the fire, Buttons awoke and had a good, long stretch. She was about to have another Big Wash when she caught sight of the gold tinsel draped over the mantelpiece. She gave it a little flick with her paw. The tinsel swayed in front of her and she couldn't resist it. She grabbed hold of it with both her front paws and it stopped swinging. Suddenly, the tinsel fell down on top of Buttons, bringing the Santa Claus ornament down with it. There was a loud crash as poor Santa landed on the floor and broke into two pieces.

Buttons ran up the stairs to escape the terrifying tinsel which had attacked her!

When Jim and Diane came home, Buttons was having a long sleep on her chair in the bedroom.

"Oh no!" exclaimed Diane. "Look at our poor Santa Claus. Buttons did not keep out of trouble!"

Sadly, she held out the ornament for Jim to see, with Santa's body in one hand and his head in the other.

"Where is that naughty cat?" asked Jim, but of course Buttons had vanished.

"I'll get the superglue to fix Santa," sighed Diane.

Santa was soon fixed almost as good as new and placed safely on top of the bookcase. Jim found some tape to stick the gold tinsel back around the mantelpiece.

"Hopefully, this will be Buttons-proof," he said.

Chapter 2

The next day was Christmas Day. When Buttons and Diane went downstairs for Operation Breakfast, they found that some exciting presents had arrived mysteriously overnight. Buttons was distracted for a moment, but soon got back to the serious business of food. Presents could wait a while.

Breakfast eaten, Buttons looked out of her cat flap ready to begin her Pussycat Patrol. She wasn't sure why, but everywhere looked different. She wondered what the strange white stuff was and bravely went out to investigate.

The white coating all over the garden gave Buttons quite a shock: it was cold! As she padded around to her front garden, Buttons was even more surprised to discover that the white stuff was not solid and her paws sank into it as she walked. Most mysterious!

A careful Patrol convinced her that the whole cul-de-sac was the same and it was white everywhere. Buttons left a trail of perfect paw prints behind her as she finished her rounds.

Back home again, Buttons found Jim and Diane finishing a special Christmas breakfast of eggs, bacon and toast. She wondered why they were not having their usual cornflakes, but didn't have long to think about it as the doorbell sounded loudly She could hear voices on the doorstep, so decided to find out what was happening. Jim was talking to the humans, Tom and Jill, from house number 2. They were visiting all their neighbours in the cul-de-sac, asking everyone to look out for their cat, Dolly, who had gone missing.

Dolly was an adult cat, but smaller than Buttons. She had beautiful fur that was covered in splodges of black, white, grey and even blue. Humans call this pattern 'tortoiseshell', but Buttons didn't know that. She did know that Dolly was also a Manx cat: like Buttons, she had a rounded bottom and no tail.

"Diane and I will have a really good search for Dolly now," Jim was saying, "and Buttons will help too, won't you?" he asked as she appeared.

Jim tickled his pet under her chin and Buttons stretched her face out for more. Jim obliged, then went upstairs to look for Dolly in case she had slipped indoors through Buttons' cat flap.

After her Big Wash, Buttons decided to go on Guard Cat Duty from the bedroom window ledge. This was a good opportunity to look out for Dolly at the same time. However, Dolly was nowhere to be seen.

As Buttons looked out, the human family from house number 5 appeared in their front garden, all wrapped up in coats, woolly hats and scarves.

Bill and Jenny also had gloves on but their children, twins Oscar and Odette, were wearing matching mittens. Buttons stared in amazement as these humans scooped up some of the strange white stuff, pressed it into balls, then threw them at each other. Buttons was surprised at this very odd game as she knew that the snow was cold. The humans didn't seem to mind and they were all laughing in their super snowball fight.

Buttons was still On Duty when Major came out for his morning walk along with his humans. Buttons felt very sorry for her dog friend who was wearing antlers and a blue, sparkly bow tie. Buttons decided that she would never be seen wearing antlers – poor Major was doing his best to ignore them!

Buttons decided that an extra Pussycat Patrol was needed, so she could look for Dolly. She set off around the cul-de-sac inspecting all the front gardens, carefully avoiding snowballs. Unfortunately, she did not find her fellow Manx cat.

Buttons went home needing a nap and a warm up after being in the snow. However, she was totally distracted from having a snooze because she heard strange crackly noises. Jim and Diane were opening their Christmas presents and Buttons jumped joyfully into the pile of torn wrapping paper. She had a marvellous time, shredding the paper and scattering it around the room. Her humans tried to get her interested in her own present, but Buttons was having far much more fun just with the torn wrapping paper.

Eventually, Diane reminded Buttons that she had a present too and Jim unwrapped it for her. It was a small box with some toys in it: a tiny red stick with green feathers on one end for her to chase, a white woollen mouse wearing a red Christmas hat and a green sparkly ball with a little bell inside it for her to play with. But Buttons wasn't interested in her presents just then as she was worn out after playing with all the wrapping paper.

"Buttons will play with her new toys later," Jim and Diane laughed.

Buttons is a clever cat and even though she had been distracted by the Christmas paper, she was determined to look for Dolly after her rest. When she awoke, she made her way to her back garden, but her Manx cat friend wasn't there.

Next Buttons explored the back garden of the house linked to her home and the large back gardens of the two bungalows at the end of the cul-de-sac. Sadly, there was no sign of Dolly.

Buttons decided to search the back gardens at the other end of the road. She started with number 8's garden, but there was no Dolly. She carried on to number 7 and then to number 6's back garden.

Suddenly Buttons heard a strange noise. She stopped to listen carefully and realised that the sound was coming from the shed. In fact, there were *several* strange noises. She had no idea what the sounds could be, so she was very cautious.

As she got nearer, she could hear high-pitched squeaking noises, lots of them. Still unsure what was making the sounds, Buttons jumped up on to the shed's window ledge.

Imagine her surprise when Buttons looked through the window and saw Dolly. Dolly was lying on her side in an empty cardboard box. She was surrounded by little balls of fur!

As Buttons looked closer, she could see that the little fur balls were moving. Buttons realised that these odd little things were making the noises, but what were they?

Buttons dropped down from the ledge and made for the shed's door. However, it was shut firmly and wouldn't open even when Buttons pushed against it with her whole body. She padded around the shed looking for any other ways to get in, but found none. There were not even any holes for a cat to squeeze through. There was no way for Buttons to get in, and no way for Dolly and the little bundles of fur to get out.

Chapter 3

Buttons was determined to rescue Dolly but realised that she needed human help to free her friend from the shed.

Buttons ran back to her own house where she found Jim in the kitchen, putting potatoes into the oven. She patted his leg, miaowing loudly.

"What's up, Buttons?" Jim asked. "Do you want a snack?"

Buttons *was* hungry, but she wanted to rescue Dolly first. She ran to the front door, but Jim didn't follow her and open it as she wanted. She patted the front door and miaowed again, but Jim still didn't understand.

"If you need to go out," he said, "you can use your cat flap."

Buttons yowled as loudly as she could. At last, this got the result she wanted and Jim came to open the front door.

"Go out then, Buttons," Jim sighed, trying to shoo her out so he could shut the door.

Refusing to budge from the doorway, Buttons turned to Jim and pawed his trouser leg.

"Hey, what are you doing? Naughty cat!" he cried.

Buttons put one paw on the doorstep and looked at Jim over her shoulder, mewling loudly.

"Ok, ok," Jim said. "I'm coming. What is the matter, Buttons?"

Of course, Buttons didn't reply, but she trotted along the path to lead Jim to house number 6, where she stood on the doorstep and miaowed again.

"What's up, Buttons?" asked Jim impatiently.

Buttons patted the front door as Jim reached down to pick her up and carry her back home. Just at that moment, Grace opened the door and was amazed to find Jim and Buttons on her doorstep. Buttons wriggled out of Jim's arms and dashed inside, making straight for their back door.

"I'm sorry, Grace, I really don't know what's up with her today," Jim apologised.

"No problem," Grace said kindly. "Come in and fetch her," she suggested.

When the humans got to Buttons, she pawed at the back door.

"Stop that!" Jim cried. "Naughty Buttons!"

"It looks like she wants us to open this door too," Grace said, puzzled. "Here you go then," she said to Buttons as she opened her back door.

Buttons went out and bounded straight over to the shed. Again she yowled as loudly as she could. Grace and

Jim were mystified, but followed her anyway. Grace opened the shed and Buttons darted inside.

"My goodness!" Grace exclaimed. "Look, it's Dolly and she's got kittens. Christmas kittens!"

"You are so clever, Buttons," Jim said. "Well done for finding Dolly!"

Grace and Jim looked together at Dolly and her kittens. There were four of them: two were tortoiseshells like Dolly; one was black and one was ginger. All except the black kitten were Manx cats matching their mum.

Buttons had never met any kittens before and she was enchanted by them. She joined Dolly in the cardboard box and enjoyed playing with the tiny cats while Jim went to fetch Tom and Jill.

Everyone was delighted that Dolly had been found and her kittens were a lovely Christmas surprise. They all called Buttons a cat superstar!

Dolly and her kittens were soon safely home, as were Buttons and Jim. Buttons ran straight to her bowl for a tasty snack as Jim told Diane what had happened.

Afterwards, Buttons went up to the bedroom and leaped onto the bed. She had loved finding Dolly and the kittens but now she needed some peace and quiet. It had been an exciting but exhausting morning.

Chapter 4

A silver car drove into the cul-de-sac, going slowly on the snow. Buttons recognised the car's engine and ran downstairs ready to greet Aunty Paula. As soon as she had said hello and merry Christmas to Diane and Jim, Paula turned to Buttons.

"I've got a little Christmas present for you," she said, reaching into her bag and pulling out a red, velvet ribbon.

Aunty Paula bent down and tied the ribbon around Buttons' neck. "That looks pretty!" Aunty Paula exclaimed.

But Buttons didn't think so! She immediately scratched at the ribbon with her claws and managed to pull it off. She turned her back on it to show that she wasn't at all impressed.

"Come on, girl," Aunty Paula said, "Where's your Christmas spirit?"

She picked up the ribbon and put it back around Buttons' neck, but she didn't even get to tie it on properly again. Buttons wriggled out of reach and escaped upstairs to the safety of Jim and Diane's bedroom with the ribbon trailing behind her.

"Never mind," Jim said. "Let's have our Christmas dinner now."

Diane, Paula and Jim sat down for a wonderful meal of roast turkey, roast potatoes, Brussels sprouts, carrots, stuffing and gravy followed by Christmas pudding and ice cream. They were all so full up after such a feast that they couldn't manage the coffee and chocolate mints afterwards. Instead, Diane turned on the television and they all sat in the living room to watch a Christmas film while they digested their fabulous food.

When Buttons crept downstairs a little while later, she was happy to discover that Diane, Jim and Aunty Paula were all asleep. Humans don't take as many afternoon naps as cats, so she was delighted with this development.

Buttons jumped up joyfully onto Aunty Paula's lap; the ribbon now forgotten. She felt very pleased with herself after rescuing Dolly *and* solving the mystery of Christmas. As she curled up ready for a welcome rest, tiny fragments of the ribbon floated up into the air and drifted over her like red velvet snowflakes.

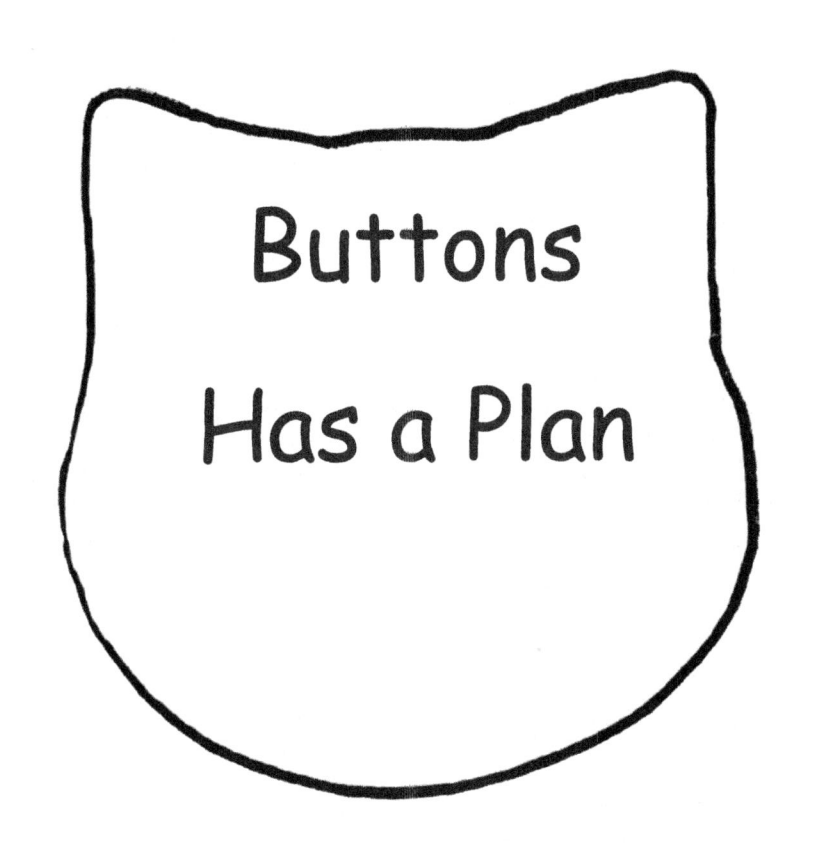

Buttons Has a Plan

5

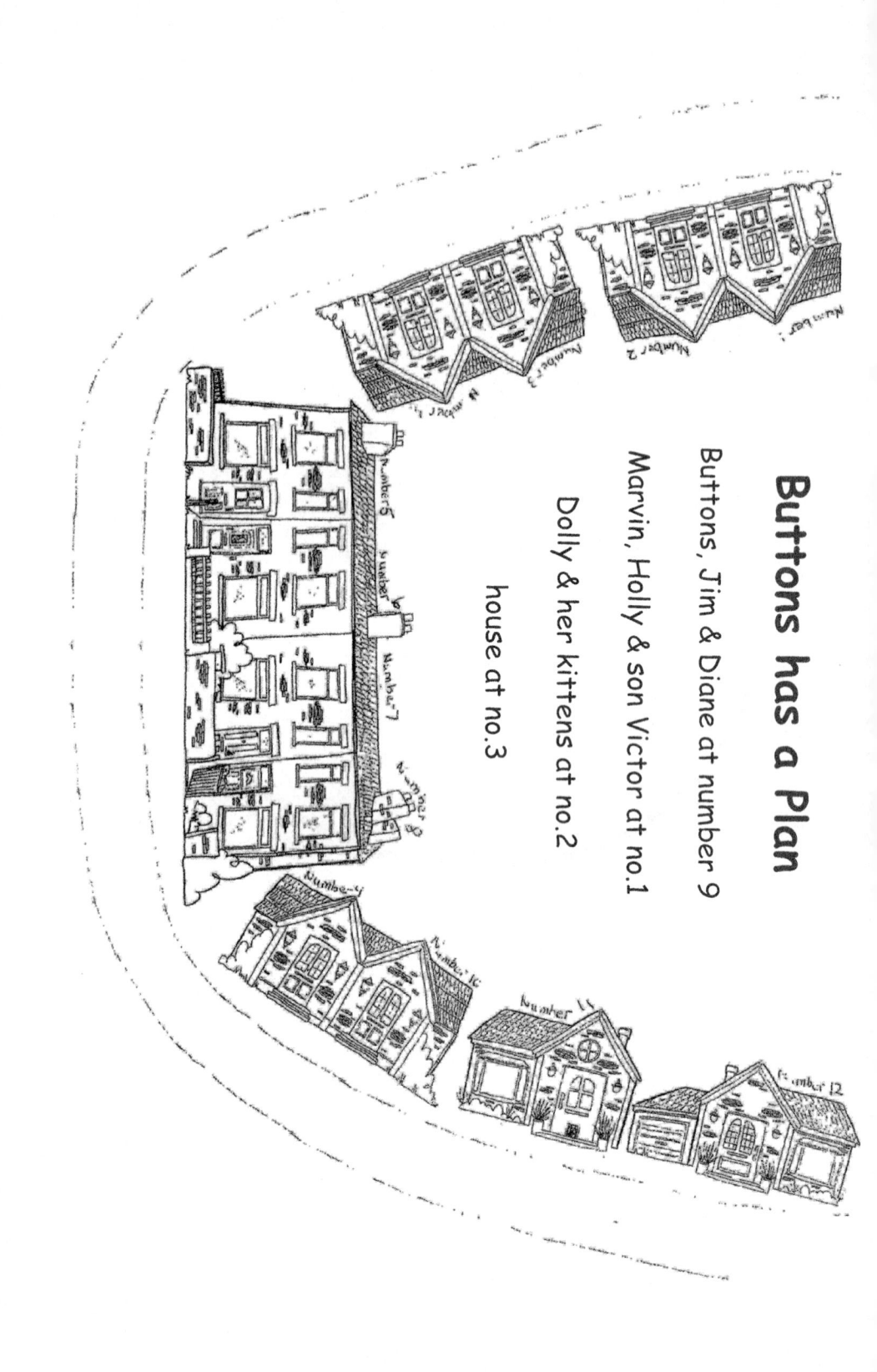

Buttons has a Plan

Buttons, Jim & Diane at number 9

Marvin, Holly & son Victor at no.1

Dolly & her kittens at no.2

house at no.3

Chapter 1

It was a gloomy morning in January. The rain was pouring and it looked set to last all day. Buttons had got very wet during one of her shortest Pussycat Patrols ever. Now she was drying off while sleeping on Diane and Jim's bed, taking absolutely no notice of the trail of muddy paw prints she had left across their new duvet cover. Buttons was warm and cosy and drying nicely and had no intention of going anywhere today!

All of a sudden, there was a noise. A strange noise. Buttons was instantly on high alert and listening carefully. She wasn't sure what the noise was, but she *was* sure that it needed investigating. She jumped down from the bed and crept cautiously down the stairs.

In the living room she had quite a surprise, for there she came face to face with another cat. Buttons wasn't at all impressed! It was Smudge, one of the two grey brothers who lived at number 7. He was named after the little patches of white fur on his forehead and the tip of his tail.

For a moment, the two cats just looked at each other, then Buttons made her move. She flew at Smudge, ready to defend her territory if she had to. Buttons was actually good friends with both of the brothers, but she didn't want any other cats in *her* house!

Smudge ran to the back door and went straight outside using the cat flap. Buttons chased him as far as her front garden, then sat by the front door quivering crossly. Smudge disappeared into his own house.

Wide awake now, Buttons glanced around the cul-de-sac. All was well, so she returned home through her cat flap and shook herself in the kitchen, scattering raindrops everywhere. Without wiping her paws on the door-mat she padded into the living room and leaped up onto the sofa. She settled herself comfortably and got back to the serious business of sleep, taking no notice at all of the muddy paw prints around her.

When Buttons woke up later that morning, she had quite forgotten all about Smudge's invasion. After eating some leftover breakfast (duck flavoured cat food), she had a thorough Big Wash then went on Guard Duty from the excellent lookout position of the window sill in the main bedroom.

Despite the torrential rain, most jobs still have to be done, so Buttons had a very busy time. First she had to supervise the soaked postman who came with a letter for Jim. Then the drenched bin men arrived and began emptying the dustbins into their truck. Even though they made a great deal of noise, Buttons wasn't afraid as she was a great Guard Cat and saw the bin men every week.

As the rain began to ease at last, the little Manx cat took note as a green van arrived at house number 11. A man got out and started unrolling a sort of rubber snake.

All cats are inquisitive and Buttons is no exception. This snake needed a thorough examination! She jumped down and made her way out of her house and carried on to number 11. She sniffed at the strange snake but she still wasn't sure what it was. She patted it but the snake didn't react. Buttons was intrigued.

Unexpectedly, the snake began to move and water squirted out of its mouth. Buttons was terrified and ran down the road to escape. She scrambled up the apple tree outside house number 1 where Marvin and Holly lived with their 8 year old son Victor. These humans had no pets of their own and Buttons climbed their tree quite often, claiming it as part of her territory. Cats don't believe that people own gardens!

Quivering on a high branch, Buttons was in time to see the man pick up the snake and aim the jet of water at the windows. She didn't understand this at all.

Buttons had never seen a window cleaner before and she was amazed by his bucket of foam, brushes and cloths. She was impressed by the man's control of the snake, as it stopped squirting water while he washed the windows and then started up again to rinse away the foamy bubbles.

The window cleaner made his way to the back of number 11 so Buttons lost sight of him as he cleaned the back windows. She continued her Guard Cat Duty as the man worked his way around the cul-de-sac.

Buttons noted which houses he visited, as not everyone had arranged for their windows to be washed today. By the time the cleaner got to house number 3, near to where she was On Duty, Buttons was so familiar with the snake that she didn't need to run away again.

As the man packed his equipment back into his van, Buttons climbed out of the tree and landed softly on the grass. She decided to visit Dolly, another little Manx cat who lived in number 2. Dolly had four kittens who were growing bigger and getting more independent every day. Buttons loved visiting Dolly and the kittens, but she found them very tiring and she soon escaped for some peace and quiet.

Chapter 2

Intending to go through her cat flap, Buttons paused by her back door. There was a strange smell coming from the back garden. Perhaps not as powerful as dogs' sense of smell, cats still have very sensitive noses. Buttons had no idea what this new scent was, so she sniffed around the flowerbeds until she found the source of the smell. It was a hedgehog!

Buttons had never met a hedgehog before and went right up to the little creature to inspect him. Of course, the hedgehog immediately curled up into a ball. Buttons didn't understand this at all and gave him a little pat with her right front paw. He was prickly! Buttons left the newcomer alone for now and sat on the damp path for an extra Big Wash to clean up her fur and paws after all that rain.

This was clever of her because she could keep an eye on the hedgehog at the same time. After a little while, he relaxed and uncurled himself. Buttons was fascinated. She approached him, but not as close as before so he didn't roll into a ball this time. Buttons got even closer and then closer still.

Eventually, the two animals were almost nose to nose. The hedgehog remained relaxed and Buttons decided that she liked this prickly little creature. They curled up together for a little snooze.

When she woke up, Buttons had a good long stretch and a thorough scratch. She decided to finish the last morsel of breakfast then have a lovely long sleep. It had been a very busy day so far.

Chapter 3

However, Buttons had a nasty surprise when she went through her cat flap. Right there, in *her* house, she found another cat! Not again, she thought crossly. But it wasn't Smudge; this time it was his totally grey brother Smoky. And Smoky was asleep, fast asleep. And he was fast asleep in **her** Radiator Slouch Pouch.

Buttons had been given the Radiator Slouch Pouch for her birthday. It was a pink, fleecy, S-shaped thing. One end was hooked over the radiator in the living room and the other end stuck out horizontally for Buttons to sleep in and be warm and cosy.

Diane had picked Buttons up and placed her in the comfy Slouch Pouch, but Buttons had always jumped right out again. So far she had refused to sleep there, but today was different. Today she had found the little grey cat in *her* Radiator Slouch Pouch. Buttons was tired and she needed a nap. And she wanted to sleep in her Slouch Pouch!

Buttons wanted Smoky to leave her house. Of course, she was still friends with him, but she wanted her Slouch Pouch back. Cats don't understand about sharing and taking turns.

First, Buttons climbed up onto the little shelf above the radiator. She miaowed but Smoky didn't move. She mewled even louder but still he didn't stir.

Next, she tried to nudge him awake. Buttons patted his grey back with her front left paw. No reaction.

She flicked his ear but still Smoky slept on.

Buttons swatted his tail. Nothing.

Then she prodded his face. Smoky snoozed on.

Finally, she tapped him right on the nose but Smoky didn't even notice.

Buttons had to stop and think. She was exhausted now and quite determined to get Smoky out of her Slouch Pouch. What she needed was a plan. A good plan. She looked around her living room and considered her options.

Spotting her box of toys which she had been given for Christmas, Buttons jumped down from the radiator shelf. A plan was beginning to form in her mind as she pulled out a white woollen mouse wearing a red Christmas hat. She carried the mouse between her teeth and returned to the radiator shelf. She dangled the toy in front of Smoky, hoping that he would wake up and want to chase it. But he paid no attention to the mouse at all.

Next Buttons tried even harder to wake Smoky up. She dropped the toy right onto his tummy but still the grey cat slept on. The mouse tumbled uselessly onto the floor.

Returning to her box of presents, Buttons changed her plan and selected a tiny red stick with green feathers on one end. Using her teeth again, she carried the stick up to the shelf above the sleeping Smoky. This time Buttons tried to tickle his face with the feathers. He twitched his nose but continued to sleep contentedly.

Buttons was feeling very tired now and she was getting cross with Smoky. Although she hadn't realised it before, the Slouch Pouch was obviously extremely comfortable and Buttons wanted it back! Thinking that a more direct approach might do the trick, Buttons carefully turned the stick around using her paws and front teeth. She clutched the feathered end in her mouth and leaned over the cat below her. She poked Smoky's back with the stick.

Two things happened as a result of this, but still her plan was unsuccessful. Firstly, Smoky stirred and moved his legs, but did not wake up. As for the second thing, Buttons' nose was irritated by the feathers and she sneezed loudly right over poor Smoky! As she sneezed, the stick fell out of her mouth and so another toy tumbled uselessly onto the floor.

Buttons jumped down once again and revised her Get Rid of Smoky Plan. With difficulty but great determination, she carried the final present up to the radiator shelf. Holding the green sparkly ball in her teeth,

Buttons leaned over and shook her head in front of Smoky's face. The little bell inside the ball jangled vigorously and at last he woke up with a horrible shock. The final straw came as the ball fell out of Buttons' mouth. It dropped onto Smoky's tummy then rolled onto the floor to join the other toys.

Feeling under attack, the frightened Smoky scrambled to escape and ran back to the safety of his own house as fast as he could.

Naughty Buttons was delighted that her plan had worked at last. She positioned herself carefully in the Slouch Pouch. Yes, it *was* warm and cosy. Lovely! With a satisfied sigh, Buttons drifted off to sleep.

Easter Buttons

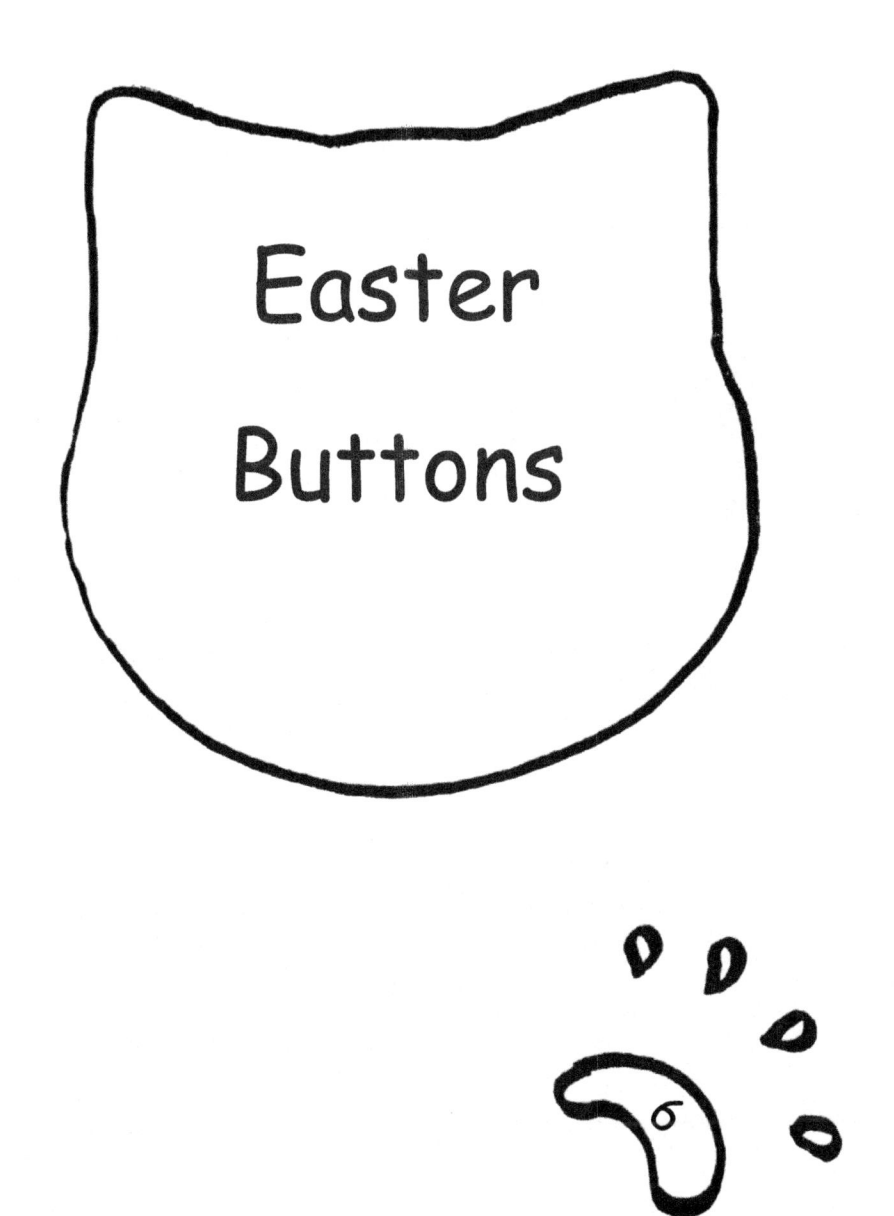

Easter Buttons

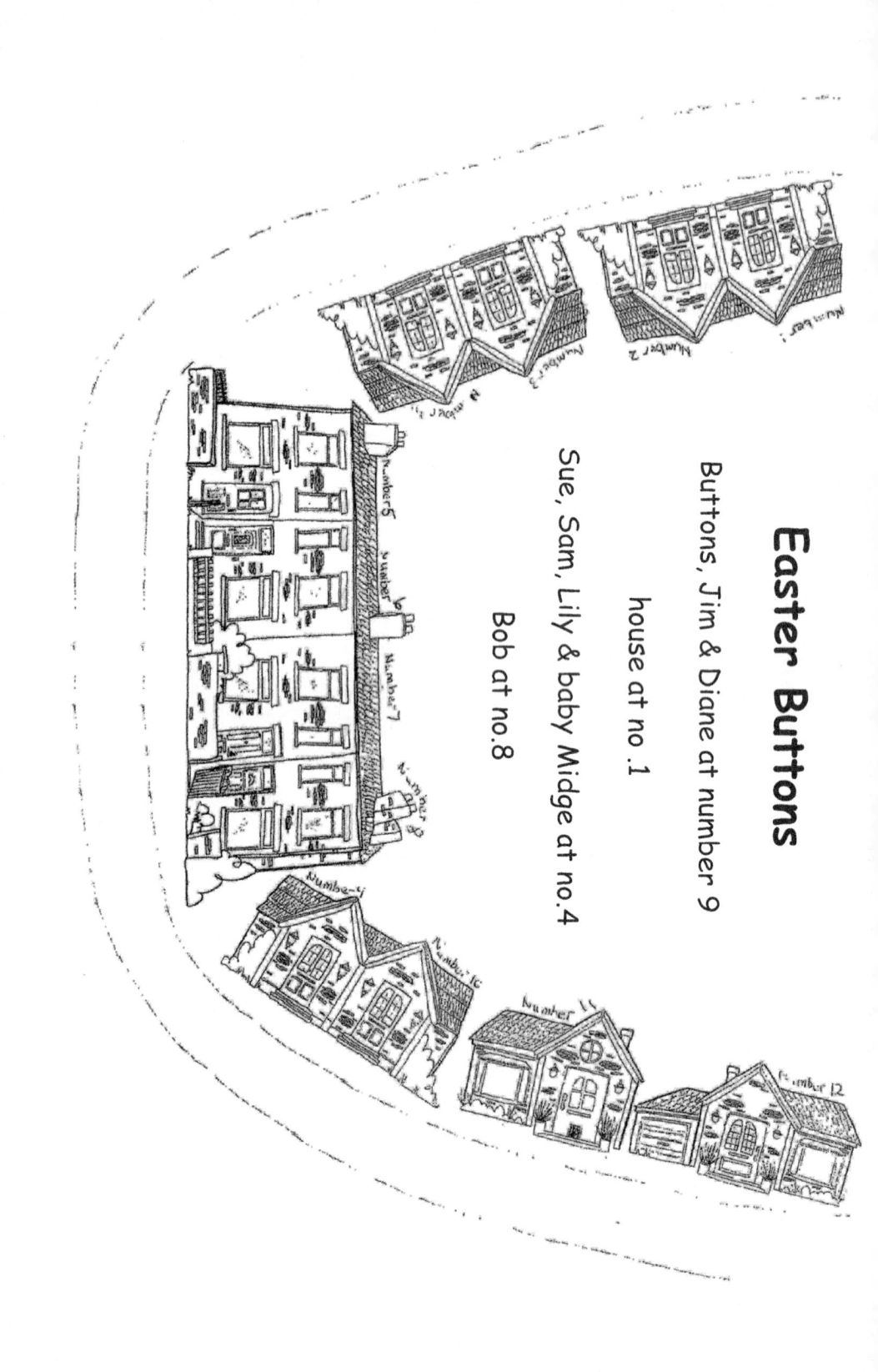

Buttons, Jim & Diane at number 9

house at no. 1

Sue, Sam, Lily & baby Midge at no. 4

Bob at no. 8

Chapter 1

After a successful Operation Breakfast and Pussycat Patrol, Buttons was having an extra nap with Diane. Poor Diane had a terrible cold and had gone back to bed after her breakfast. Buttons was delighted with this development and wondered if she could train Diane to sleep more every day.

It was a Saturday in April. Buttons didn't know that it was the Saturday before Easter Sunday. Jim was out doing the shopping and he had some special things for Easter in his trolley: chocolate eggs, fluffy toy chicks and a beautiful bunch of daffodils. He also had all the ingredients he needed to bake a cake.

When he got home with several bulging bags of shopping, Buttons woke up and went downstairs. She got busy with her Big Wash while keeping an eye on Jim. He started unpacking his bags and Buttons was amazed to see several large eggs in shiny blue, red, green and gold. She had never seen such big eggs before and was sure that egg shells did not usually have such bright colours.

"These are not for you," Jim told her as he noticed her interest in them. "They are for Diane and Aunty Paula."

Jim put the chocolate eggs on the dining table, right on the far side so that Buttons could not easily reach them. He put the daffodils in two vases of water, placing them on the dining table as well, ready to decorate the house for the Easter lunch he would be cooking tomorrow.

Hearing the postman on his rounds, Buttons set off through her cat flap for an extra Pussycat Patrol.

Jim made himself a cup of tea and took one upstairs for Diane. Poor Diane was feeling awful.

"Don't worry about a thing," said Jim. "I've already got all the shopping and now I will go and bake a special Easter cake. You stay in bed and hopefully you will be well enough to enjoy our lunch with Paula tomorrow."

In the kitchen, Jim started weighing out ingredients. He put butter and sugar in a large bowl and mixed them together. He added eggs and flour, then mixed in some sultanas and cinnamon. Jim spooned the mixture into a prepared baking tin and put it in the oven to bake.

Feeling very pleased with himself, Jim set about decorating the living room. He chose the best places to put the chocolate eggs and the fluffy toy chicks. Carefully he placed one vase of daffodils on the mantelpiece over the fireplace and put the other on the coffee table. Finally, he took the special rabbit-shaped plate out of the cupboard and put it in pride of place on the coffee table next to the daffodils.

"The house looks perfect for Easter," Jim muttered to himself, gazing with pleasure at his handiwork.

The cat flap swung open and shut again as Buttons returned.

"Look here," Jim said, pointing to the plate, "it's the Easter Bunny!"

Buttons did take a look but she was not impressed. Of course, the plate was flat. Even worse, the rabbit was wearing a blue shirt and red trousers. He was like no bunny that she had ever seen!

Jim went to the kitchen to check on the cake. It was rising nicely but wasn't ready yet. He sat down on the sofa to read his newspaper.

Buttons climbed into her Radiator Slouch Pouch for a welcome nap. As she turned to make herself comfortable, she spotted something odd on the bookcase. It was yellow and fluffy and about the same size as a melon. Buttons was certain that it had not been there before and she was intrigued.

Cats are very agile, so it was easy for her to jump on top of the bookcase from her Slouch Pouch. She landed softly next to the strange thing. Jim was busy reading and so he didn't see what happened next.

Buttons patted the yellow thing and it fell silently off the bookcase. However, Buttons took fright and leaped away for safety. She landed on the coffee table but it wasn't as safe as it usually was. She bumped into the vase and it fell over with a thud. Luckily it did not break but the flowers and water spilled out over Jim's feet and onto the carpet.

Jim cried out in surprise as his feet got wetter and wetter. He looked around for the culprit, but Buttons was nowhere to be seen!

Jim dashed into the kitchen to fetch some tea towels and began clearing up the mess. Unfortunately, he was so busy that he forgot all about the cake.

When Jim returned to the kitchen to put some fresh water in the vase and put the tea towels in the washing machine, he could smell burning.

He took the cake out of the oven and put it on the cooling rack. Poor Jim. He had been so proud of his baking and was very disappointed now. However, once the cake was cool enough to turn out of its baking tin, Jim realised that it wasn't so bad after all. Only the top and sides were a bit burned, so Jim sliced off the top and was happy to discover that the cake top now looked fine.

After that, Jim tried to cut away the sides of the cake. This turned out to be a bit of a disaster! The round cake ended up looking like a mangled, lopsided hexagon, and no amount of cutting was able to even it up again. Jim decided to make it a square instead and this worked well.

Jim made some icing and drizzled it over his Easter cake. He was relieved that it looked so lovely! He placed it carefully on a plate and put it in a large cake tin so that nothing else could go wrong with it.

Then he looked at the pieces of cake which he had cut off. Jim knew that some of these were burnt, but some slices were only the cut-offs from where he had tried to reproduce the circular shape.

"Maybe the birds will eat some of this," Jim mumbled to himself as he crumbled the cake into tiny pieces. He brushed all the crumbs into a bowl and then threw them under the tree in the front garden.

Meanwhile, Buttons had taken refuge under the apple tree of house number 1. She wasn't at all pleased to see Jim throwing cake crumbs over *her* garden! Even worse, some sparrows flew down and began eating. A starling joined them and Buttons could bear it no longer!

She bounded over to her garden, scattering the birds in all directions. Then she took up her Guard Cat position under the bush near the front door.

After a little while, some of the birds returned.

"Humans!" she thought sadly as she considered how to solve the problem that Jim had created.

The answer came to her in a flash. Stepping onto the grass, she started eating up the cake pieces *herself!* Jim was astounded when he looked out of the window to see his little cat among all the crumbs.

"What are you doing, Buttons?" he asked, opening the front door. "If I had put some cake in your food dish, you would have refused to eat it. Silly cat!" he laughed.

Cats get very offended if they are laughed at. Buttons ignored her human and strode off haughtily to the back garden. Jim would just have to deal with the situation without her help, she thought!

Chapter 2

Easter Sunday was sunny and fresh, one of those beautiful days full of the promise of the summer to come. Poor Dine had coughed and sneezed so often that she had slept very badly the night before. Jim and Buttons had slept badly too, in fact Buttons was exhausted.

So, the little cat was having an extra-long rest after her usual morning tasks. She lay curled up in the plant pot which stood by the front doormat on the opposite side to her scratching post. She had taken to snoozing here since Diane had planted some daffodil bulbs a few weeks ago. Bob from house number 8 had laughed when he first saw her there.

"Where did you buy the cat plant?" he joked with Diane. "It looks just like a real cat!"

Buttons had ignored the joke because the plant pot had been quite a cosy spot for a nap when the sun warmed up the compost. It had the added advantage of being an excellent look-out position when she was on Guard Cat Duty.

However, the daffodil bulbs were beginning to shoot up and Buttons had trodden them down so that she could get comfortable. Luckily, neither of her humans had noticed.

Buttons opened one eye as she heard footsteps in the cul-de-sac. She recognised the newspaper delivery boy, but he had no papers for Diane and Jim so her supervision was not needed today. Feeling assured that all was well, the little cat settled back to sleep.

But Buttons was soon awoken by voices further up the cul-de-sac. She looked round to see Sue from house number 4 putting baby Midge into his pushchair. The baby was chuckling happily with his siblings Sam and Lily as they all set off. Buttons was intrigued. They went by car to school and she had already solved that mystery, so where were they going?

Sue didn't notice that Buttons was following them. She was too busy chatting to Sam and Lily and pointing things out to baby Midge (a green car, a sparrow and the red post-box on the corner).

Buttons trailed after them when they turned left out of the cul-de-sac. She had never been this way before and was enjoying all the new sights. When they came to a road, Sue looked carefully to the right, then left and then right again. When it was clear, they all crossed the road safely and carried on walking.

Buttons had never seen such a busy road and she didn't like the cars and the noise they made. Her cul-de-sac was much quieter and safer. She paused for a moment on the pavement then suddenly dashed across. She didn't look in either direction first; sadly cats do not have any road crossing sense. Luckily, she avoided trouble and bounded after her neighbours.

Buttons found herself in a playpark. Midge was laughing as Sue pushed him to and fro in a baby swing. Sam and Lily ran over to their favourite, the shiny purple seesaw. There were other children in the park too and Buttons wandered around quite fascinated by the slide, roundabout and climbing frame. She particularly liked the little play collection of zoo animals on enormous springs for children to bounce on. She jumped onto an elephant's back, but she wasn't heavy enough to make it bounce.

It was then that Buttons had a nasty shock. She looked everywhere in the park, but Sue and her children were gone! Even worse, Buttons was not sure which way was the right way to go home. There were four gates into the park and Buttons couldn't remember which one they had all come through. Poor Buttons was lost!

Buttons chose a gate and stepped through it, looking around uncertainly. A big lorry thundered past and terrified the little cat. She ran back into the park as quickly as she could and hid under a park bench. Her heart was beating very fast and she trembled all over. Poor Buttons!

Once the noisy monster lorry had gone, Buttons slinked silently through another gate. She still wasn't at all sure where she was or which direction was the right way home. But then she thought she could see a familiar car. It was just like Jim's car and it was parked under a big tree. Unfortunately, Jim was nowhere to be seen. Deciding to wait for him, Buttons clambered up onto the car's bonnet.

That was when she had another nasty shock. A horrible loud wailing sound started up. Terrified once more, Buttons leaped into the tree and scrambled up as high as she could.

A man came out of a nearby house and pressed a button on his key fob to turn off the alarm. He gazed around to discover who had set his car alarm off, but no-one was near it. Then he noticed the cat paw prints on his bonnet. He looked all about again, but couldn't see a cat anywhere.

Meanwhile, Buttons had a big problem. In her terror, she had climbed up high into the tree, but now she was stuck. Cats are very good at climbing *up* but they cannot climb down facing forwards like squirrels. Buttons began mewling miserably.

The car's owner looked up when he heard poor Buttons' cries. He saw an unhappy and frightened pair of cat's eyes looking down at him.

"Oh no, you are really high up there!" he exclaimed. "Don't worry, I will get you some help."

And so, a short time later a fire engine arrived and parked near the big tree. Buttons was too scared already to be frightened by its loud engine and flashing red and blue lights. The firemen put up a ladder and one firefighter climbed up but Buttons was still out of reach.

Down on the ground a small crowd was forming and everyone watched as the firefighters extended their ladder even more. Despite her fears, the fireman spoke soft words of encouragement and slowly Buttons crept forward to his outstretched arms. A little cheer went up from the crowd as Buttons was carried down to safety.

A woman wearing black jeans and a pink tee-shirt stepped out from the crowd with her camera. She took several photographs of Buttons in the fireman's arms. The best photo was the one with the ladder and the tree in the background. The fireman was smiling and Buttons was very glad to be rescued. The lady took down a few details in her notebook.

"This will make a great story for my newspaper," the smiling reporter said.

Suddenly a familiar voice sounded from the crowd: "I know that cat. It's Buttons!"

It was Granny – hooray! The reporter took another photo as Granny took Buttons from the fireman and placed her safely in her shopping basket. Granny carried her along the street towards home. It was a bit of a bumpy ride for Buttons but she didn't mind!

As they turned into the cul-de-sac, Buttons leaped out of the basket. She walked proudly home by Granny's side.

Chapter 3

Jim had been very busy, preparing vegetables and roasting beef for the special lunch. Fortunately, Diane was feeling a bit better and was able to enjoy the meal with Jim and Paula *and* Granny.

The women were impressed with Jim's cooking and his house decorating. Buttons joined them in the living room and curled up on Aunty Paula's lap as Jim brought in the cake.

"Ta daa!", Jim exclaimed, showing off his cake creation.

He cut a slice for all the humans and offered a small taste to Buttons. The little cat ignored it.

"This cake is delicious," said Aunty Paula, wiping her fingers on a napkin.

"So clever of you to make an unusual square cake!" Granny added.

Buttons looked at Jim, but he only smiled.

Later that afternoon, Diane, Paula and Granny had a mini-Treasure Hunt for chocolate eggs. Jim had placed them around the living room and they weren't actually hard to find, but it was a good game anyway. -Diane unwrapped an egg and Buttons appeared from the garden. She sniffed at the chocolate but wasn't tempted to taste it.

Instead, she had a great game of Chase with the shiny wrappers which the humans rolled into little balls for her.

After so much activity, the black and white cat was exhausted. Once again, she climbed onto Aunty Paula's lap, yawning widely. Yes, a good long snooze was what she needed.

A few days later, Jim sat down to relax after work with the local newspaper.

"Look, Diane," he said, showing her the front page. "Buttons is in the news!"

Buttons enjoyed being the centre of attention as everyone in the cul-de-sac read the news of the star cat of the neighbourhood. It was great fun to be famous, but also very tiring. Buttons loved adventures, and would certainly have more as she solved new mysteries, but for now a nice nap was in order. Soon she was asleep, dreaming of enormous eggs in bright, shiny colours.

Buttons And the TT

Buttons and the TT

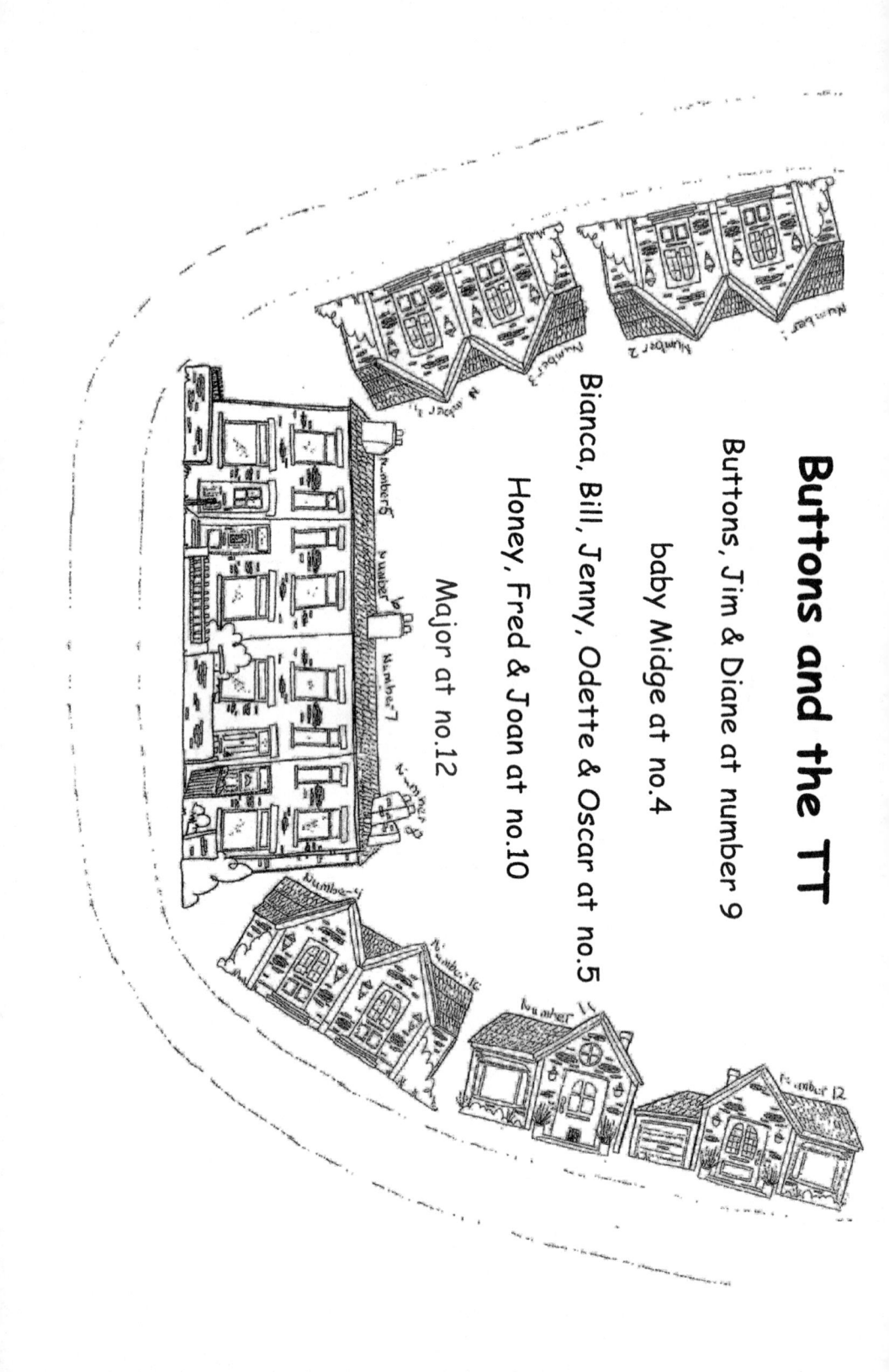

Buttons, Jim & Diane at number 9

baby Midge at no.4

Bianca, Bill, Jenny, Odette & Oscar at no.5

Honey, Fred & Joan at no.10

Major at no.12

Chapter 1

Buttons was lying on the bed in the spare bedroom, curled up in a warm, sunny spot. She was quite contented after a good Operation Breakfast (cod flavour cat food served up by Diane), an uneventful Pussycat Patrol and a thorough Big Wash. Now Buttons was dreaming happily about chasing a pair of large white mice, one of whom was wearing a red Santa hat! She awoke with a start, allowing her dream mice to escape.

There was a sudden loud noise as a machine arrived in the cul-de-sac. Buttons recognised the throbbing roar of the engine and she was delighted. She dashed downstairs and was soon going out through her cat flap and trotting off to find the source of the noise.

As she came around the side of her house, she saw that she was right. It was a motorbike, a red, shiny motorbike. Buttons was overjoyed: she loved motorbikes!

The bike rider and his pillion passenger took off their leather gloves and put them on the bike's seat while they unstrapped their crash helmets. Buttons was there in time to help them put their gloves inside their helmets and place them carefully down on the ground.

The female newcomer gave Buttons a stroke and rang the doorbell of house number 10 while her husband unloaded their panniers, the luggage which can be attached to the sides and back of a motorbike.

When Fred and Joan opened the door, their dog Honey rushed outside. She raced around the bikers, jumping up and barking excitedly. Everyone, including Buttons, went inside. The guests were Jason, Fred and Joan's son, and his wife Ava. The humans had lots to talk about while they drank coffee. The two animals had new laps to sit on and new people to stroke them.

Jason and Ava were not the only people to come to the island for a holiday. Visitors were flocking to the Isle of Man by ferry or by plane. There was a buzz of excitement as everyone got ready for the TT, the famous motorcycle road races.

After a while, Buttons heard a car arriving in front of her house. It wasn't a car she recognised, so she had to investigate. She jumped down from Jason's comfortable knees and made her way to the front door. She waited impatiently, scratching the door as Joan came to open it for her.

"Ok, Queen Buttons. I'm here now obeying your command! Goodbye," laughed Joan.

Buttons left the house next door without saying thank you. Cats have no idea about human manners! She was eager to see who had come to visit her; there was no doubt in her mind that the new arrivals had come to visit *her* rather than her humans!

There was a yellow car on her drive which Buttons had never seen before. Diane was there too, helping to unload the boot. First she took out a large bag and carried it indoors. Next she took in a changing mat and a soft, mauve blanket. Finally she unloaded a carrycot and took that inside as well.

"Is this everything you need for Carla?" Diane asked her friend.

"One more bag on the front seat, please," Cathy replied.

Buttons was amazed. She wondered who could possibly need so much equipment. She got her answer as Cathy held out a little bundle to Diane.

It was a baby, a tiny baby. Buttons often saw baby Midge from house number 4, but this baby was much smaller. She was rather wrinkly and her skin was very pink. The little cat was fascinated by this tiny girl. She had no idea that someone so small could need so much baggage!

"She's beautiful," said Diane, cradling the infant in her arms. "And you are now a big brother, Kevin!" she added.

It was then that Buttons saw a toddler being unstrapped from his car seat. The little boy was wearing blue shorts and a t-shirt with a boat on it. His hair was sandy coloured.

The toddler was entranced by Buttons and reached out to pull lightly on one of her ears. His mum, Cathy, showed him how to stroke her silky fur, which Buttons definitely preferred.

"No tail!" Kevin exclaimed excitedly, as he stroked Buttons from her head to the little furry tuft on her bottom.

"You are so clever to notice that," said Diane. "Buttons is a Manx cat, so she was born without a tail. The old story goes that when Noah was calling all the animals to come onto the Ark, the two Manx cats were too busy sleeping. It was only as Noah started to shut the doors that they woke up and ran as fast as they could to get on board. They made it just in time but their tails got stuck in the doors and got left behind. That's why Manx cats don't have tails!" she explained.

Kevin was most interested in the story but little Buttons wasn't listening. Like all cats, she considered herself to be absolutely perfect.

Once everyone was indoors, Diane made tea and poured a glass of milk for Kevin. The toddler was busily exploring house number 9. He found Buttons' box of toys and was soon playing with her toy mouse wearing the red Christmas hat.

Buttons didn't mind and she was enchanted by the baby anyway. She climbed onto the sofa where Cathy was sitting with her daughter in her arms. Buttons peered at the baby, getting closer and closer until she was nose to nose with her.

As Buttons watched, the baby screwed up her eyes and began to wail. Quick as a flash Buttons jumped away from the horrible sound. She had no idea that someone so small could make so much noise!

Buttons joined Kevin and the two new friends had a wonderful game of Pit-Pat with Buttons' sparkly ball. It was an odd game as Buttons was so much faster than Kevin and Kevin was happy to chase Buttons rather than the ball. Kevin grabbed a little fistful of her fur but she didn't mind – somehow, Buttons understood that Kevin was only a youngster and meant her no harm.

Diane heated some milk for the baby and the crying soon stopped. Then the baby needed to be winded and was a little bit sick. Cathy cleaned her up and then she changed her nappy. Babies are hard work, thought Buttons.

Poor Kevin was soon bored. Diane noticed and said that new Big Brothers deserved a treat. She scooped some ice cream into a cone for him and opened the back door so that Kevin and Buttons could explore the back garden.

After a few minutes Buttons came back in and sat down on the rug. She had ice cream all around her mouth and over her whiskers! Buttons licked as much of the tasty ice cream as she could, then set about washing her face. The two women laughed but Buttons took no notice.

After the guests had gone home, Buttons needed an extra-long rest. She loved having visitors and was especially pleased to be friends with Kevin; he was welcome to come again, she thought. However, she was now very tired and settled down on a deckchair in the back garden for a nap while Diane sat on the other deckchair to read a book. Both of them enjoyed the peace and quiet after Cathy had taken her children home.

Chapter 2

Buttons was dreaming contentedly about motorbikes and awoke to realise that her dream was coming true. Another bike was arriving in the cul-de-sac. Immediately, she scampered round to the front gardens to see where this bike was going. She saw it pull up in front of house number 5.

As Buttons darted over to greet this new bike and its rider, she was surprised to see Bianca running towards her, trembling in terror. Poor Bianca rushed to hide at the other end of the road. She chose the back garden of house number 12, where the golden Labrador Major was snoozing in the sunshine. The little white cat curled up with her doggy friend for extra protection.

Buttons decided to try and help Bianca, but not just now. Now she needed to supervise this new arrival. The motorbike was black with a light brown leather seat in the triangular shape of a bicycle seat. Buttons had no way of knowing that this was a vintage bike, but she definitely loved the roar of its engine and the smell from the bike's oil. She jumped up joyfully onto the seat as the rider climbed off and set the bike on its stand.

As the man took off his gloves and helmet, Bill and Jenny opened their front door. They were just in time to see him pick up Buttons and place her gently on the ground.

"This rotten cat is obviously a fan of the TT," the newcomer said crossly, "but she's **not** allowed to sit on my old Beauty!"

The twins were there too and they giggled as their uncle Stephen lovingly patted his vintage motorcycle. As they all entered the house, Buttons strode haughtily away, pretending that it had been *her* idea to get off the motorbike. Of Bianca, their own cat, there was no sign.

As the afternoon drew to a close, Buttons went home to conduct Diane's Teatime Training. This went very well and she was soon tucking into a portion of duck flavoured cat food.

She climbed onto the sofa and was cleaning up her whiskers when Jim returned home. Naughty Buttons ran to him and twirled around his ankles, miaowing for food, but her ruse was foiled when Diane announced that Buttons had already been fed.

During her evening Pussycat Patrol, Buttons found Bianca cautiously approaching her own home. The beautiful white cat was very nervous because the old bike was parked by her front door.

Buttons took several steps towards Bianca's house, then turned and looked back at Bianca over her shoulder. Bianca started to follow Buttons, but she was too afraid to walk up the path where she thought that the strange black machine was waiting to eat her. Poor Bianca!

Buttons patted the bike's back wheel as Bianca watched, then she jumped right up onto its black petrol tank. Bianca trembled at Buttons' bravery, but was encouraged to come closer when Buttons didn't get eaten!

Luckily Stephen wasn't watching as Buttons walked along the top of his motorbike and stood on its seat, purring loudly. Bianca grew more confident and was able to pass the bike and go into her house through her cat flap. Buttons was pleased with her success.

Buttons leaped onto the path and patrolled right around the motorcycle. There was a metal tray under the engine, collecting small drips of oil. Buttons peered closer and several little drops fell onto her head. Buttons loved the smell so she was quite happy with this.

When she got home, however, Jim insisted on washing the oil away, much to Buttons' dismay.

"We can't let you lick the oil when you are having your next Big Wash," he told the cat who was doing her best to wriggle away from him.

As soon as she was clean, Jim released her and Buttons escaped outside through her cat flap. She saw that Bianca had conquered her fear and was having a little nap on her doorstep, right next to the old motorbike. Buttons was very proud of her.

Feeling rather tired herself, Buttons jumped onto the seat of the shiny, red bike outside the house next door. If any more bikes arrived in the cul-de-sac, perhaps she could teach *all* the neighbourhood cats to love them! With this happy thought, Buttons lay down, curled up and closed her eyes and fell fast asleep.

Buttons in Love!

Buttons in Love!

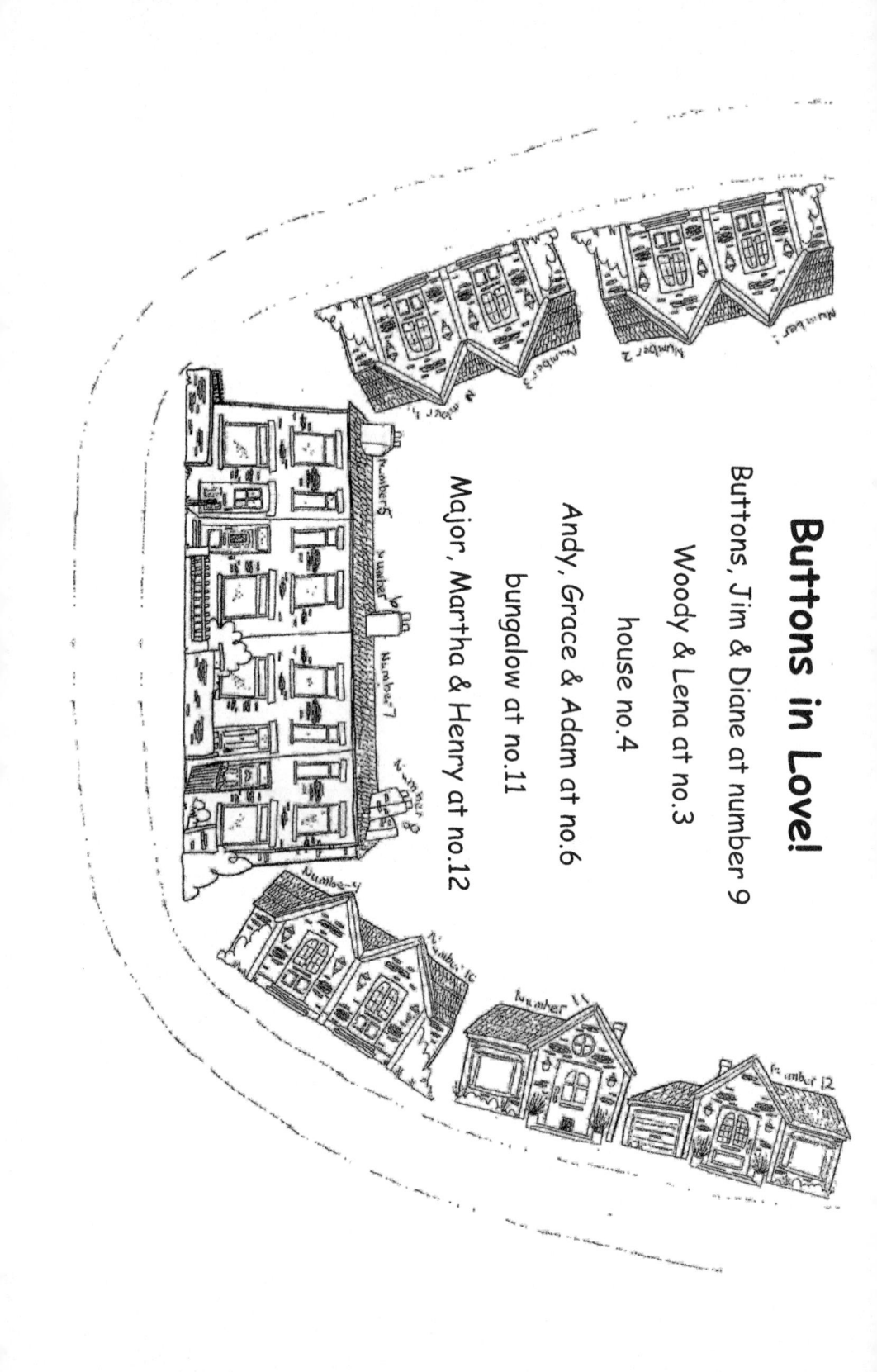

Buttons, Jim & Diane at number 9

Woody & Lena at no.3

house no.4

Andy, Grace & Adam at no.6

bungalow at no.11

Major, Martha & Henry at no.12

Chapter 1

Outside it was cold and frosty, but Buttons was warm and cosy. She was snuggled up in bed with Jim and Diane. The humans were sleeping under their duvet and the little Manx cat was lying on top of it. Buttons was on her side with all four of her legs stretched out. She had lots of room, whereas her owners were reduced to a slither of the bed on each side of her.

Diane was the first of them all to wake up. She got out of bed, put on her dressing gown and slippers, popped into the bathroom then headed downstairs. In the kitchen, she put the kettle on and looked around for her pet but Buttons wasn't there. Buttons was reluctant to leave the warmth of the bed, but her tummy was rumbling so she decided to get up and go downstairs for her breakfast after all.

"You are late today, Snugglepuss," laughed Diane. "It is chilly so we will leave the heating on for you today."

Buttons didn't understand about heating, but she was very glad that the house was warm and toasty. After a tuna flavoured portion of cat food, she peered out of her cat flap before going outside. She didn't like the icy frost on her paws, so she had a super-quick Pussycat Patrol, noting nothing out of order and dashing back indoors. She climbed into her Radiator Slouch Pouch to warm herself up again.

After a thorough Big Wash, Buttons went on Guard Cat Duty on the living room window ledge. She took note as Major, the golden Labrador from the bungalow at number 12, went past for his morning walk with his human called Martha. Some cats and dogs do not get along, but Buttons and Major were great friends. Sometimes Buttons even went in the bungalow and helped Martha or her husband Henry find their fridge. Then she would sit next to the fridge and miaow

until someone opened it and found a meaty treat for her. This might have been rather cheeky, but both animals approved as Major always got a treat too.

Her next Guard Cat duty was to supervise the postman on his rounds. Buttons observed which homes had mail today, then yawned widely. Just another careful glance around the whole cul-de-sac, then it would be time for a little rest.

It was then that she got her first glimpse of a stranger. There was a new cat in the neighbourhood!

This new cat was ginger. He had stripes of a darker shade of ginger and his eyes were green. He was striding purposefully around the cul-de-sac. Buttons didn't know where he had come from or where he was going. Despite the frost, she had to investigate this newcomer.

Cautiously, she went outside and set off after him. The ginger cat took absolutely no notice of her at all. Buttons followed him until the recycling truck arrived. Two men got out and started collecting the used paper, card, tins, plastic and glass. Buttons was a great Guard Cat and had seen these men lots of times. She wasn't afraid of the noise they made, not even when the glass jars and bottles smashed into the back of the lorry.

However, the ginger cat had obviously never seen a recycling truck before and the noise scared him. He ran and hid under Nick and Beth's car which was parked outside their bungalow at number 11.

Buttons gazed under the car at the ginger cat quivering there. For a moment the two cats just looked at each other, then Buttons turned away and went home. She let herself in through her cat flap and bounded up onto the window sill again so that she could supervise the recycling collectors on their way along her road. It was then that she heard the unmistakeable sound of her cat flap opening again and swinging shut once more.

Chapter 2

Buttons looked around to see the ginger cat stepping into *her* house! There was another loud crash outside from the recycling glass tipping into the truck. The ginger tom hid under the dining table.

Buttons was a very friendly cat. She was on good terms with all the other animals in the cul-de-sac and was a firm favourite with all the humans too. She loved meeting newcomers and she always thought that visitors to Jim and Diane's house were there to see her rather than her humans. However, she did *not* like other cats coming into **her** house!

Jumping down onto the carpet, Buttons trotted over to the dining table. Once again, the pair of cats looked at each other. Something strange happened then. Buttons found herself admiring the tom's deep green eyes, while the visitor was entranced by Buttons' silky black fur with the white patches. He particularly liked her right front paw, white with the black spot on it, just like a button.

Buttons decided to eat some of her leftover breakfast. She took several paces towards the kitchen, then stopped and looked back at the tom cat over her shoulder. The new cat understood her invitation to join her and soon both of them were eating up the remains of the tuna flavoured cat food.

After that the guest went out through the cat flap with Buttons watching him adoringly. Feeling very sleepy now, Buttons climbed into her Slouch Pouch for a nice nap.

That evening, Granny came to visit. As Jim opened the front door for her, Buttons ran to greet Granny too. She always had some cat treats in her pocket and the little cat loved her Granny.

"You spoil her," Jim and Diane laughed as Buttons tapped Granny's leg for another cat biscuit.

"Buttons is a lovely cat and she deserves some treats!" Granny exclaimed.

Buttons agreed wholeheartedly with this.

"Anyway," she continued, "I've got some treats for you two as well."

Granny gave Jim a bag of scones which were still warm from her oven.

"Fantastic!" Jim sighed happily as he buttered three of them and spread strawberry jam on top. Everyone appreciated their tasty snack.

"We will leave the other scones on the worktop to cool down. We'll enjoy them tomorrow," Diane said as she put the rest of the scones on a plate with a tea towel over them.

Buttons had a little snooze on Granny's lap while Diane showed her the blue jumper she was knitting for Jim's birthday. Granny was impressed with her progress, as Diane was quite new to knitting. Then the humans watched a dancing competition on the television.

Cats are not much interested in dancing so after a while, Buttons went outside for an evening Pussycat Patrol. Would she get a glimpse of the gorgeous ginger cat?

When the adverts came on, Jim went into the kitchen to make all the humans a cup of tea. He was most surprised to find the ginger cat on the worktop. Even worse, the tea towel was on the floor and the stranger was busily eating the scones!

Buttons was there too, sitting on the floor next to the tea towel, gazing up in admiration.

"Come quick and see this!" Jim cried. "There is a ginger cat in our kitchen!"

Diane and Granny were just in time to see a flash of ginger fur as the tom cat escaped through the cat flap.

"Wow!" gasped Diane admiringly. "He's as fast as a Ninja. Just look at him go – he's a really handsome Ginger Ninja!"

"And why were you just sitting there and watching him?" Jim asked Buttons. "You should have chased him out."

"Buttons is in love!" said Granny, as Buttons gazed adoringly after the handsome stranger.

Everyone laughed and Buttons strode haughtily into the dining room. Cats are very dignified creatures and hate to be laughed at.

Meanwhile Jim was examining the scones.

"They **all** have bite marks," he stated sadly, "and these two have been licked as well. The Ginger Ninja didn't spare any of the scones for us!"

"Never mind," said Granny kindly. "I will crumble them up to feed to the ducks in the park tomorrow. I'll bake you some more scones at the weekend and I'll put them in a cat-proof tin."

Then they set about cleaning up. Diane washed the plate while Granny wiped down the worktop. Jim fetched the vacuum cleaner from the cupboard under the stairs.

As soon as she saw the vacuum cleaner, Buttons vanished through the cat flap as well. She had never actually been attacked by it, but she hated its noise and its vibrations. She wasn't going to give it the chance to get her.

"Poor Buttons," Diane said. "Her new boyfriend has disgraced himself and now she has to run away from the Cat Eating Machine!"

Chapter 3

The next day was still cold though the sun shone weakly over the Isle of Man. Buttons had successfully completed all her morning jobs and would normally have been feeling quite pleased with herself now. But not today. Today she had been hoping to meet her new friend again, but so far, the ginger tom was nowhere to be seen.

Suddenly the peace of the morning was shattered by barking. Buttons was instantly on high alert. She wondered what was going on.

Realising that the noise was coming from Woody, her Dalmatian dog friend from house number 3, Buttons cautiously crept along the road to see if the situation needed her help. It did!

There was a man there, a man new to the neighbourhood. He had a blue tartan shopping trolley and as Buttons approached, he took something out of his trolley and tried to push it through the letterbox. Woody, on the other side of the door, grabbed it between his teeth and started pulling.

Perhaps the man should have just left it there and continued on to the next house, but he didn't. He started pulling the leaflet back again. For a few moments he had quite a tug-of-war with Woody until the leaflet suddenly ripped, sending him flying backwards.

As Lena opened her front door she was met with an astonishing sight. Buttons had leaped onto the man's trolley and was looking down on him in triumph. He sat up, still clutching his torn half of the leaflet, a dazed look on his face.

"Oh dear," said Lena, "I am so sorry. Woody is a very friendly dog really. Would you like to come in and meet him?" she asked.

The man got up hurriedly and gave Lena his half of the leaflet. Buttons jumped down from the trolley and went into the house. The two animals stood side-by-side looking out of the front door, Woody still biting his half of the leaflet.

"Er, n, no thanks," the man stammered, "not today. I must get back to my delivering."

Brushing his trousers down with one hand, he took hold of his trolley with the other and rushed away to the next house. He continued round the cul-de-sac, trying to regain his composure and dignity.

Lena closed the door and turned to see Buttons trotting into the kitchen with Woody at her heels. Buttons patted the fridge and Lena laughed.

"Ok, I think you do both deserve a treat. Well done for saving me from the leaflet man!" exclaimed Lena.

She gave them both a piece of cooked chicken, kindly deciding to have a jam sandwich for her lunch instead. Then Buttons did a quick tour of the house before Lena opened the back door for her to go out.

Buttons did not go straight home, however. She heard voices and was surprised to see Jim and Diane on the doorstep of house number 6. Of course, the little Manx cat had to investigate.

The mystery was solved when she heard Andy and Grace explaining that their teenage son, Adam, was looking after the ginger cat while his owners were on holiday. The tom's real name was revealed to be Douglas, but Diane and Jim preferred to call him the Ginger Ninja!

Chapter 4

Although he wasn't going to be in the neighbourhood for very long, Douglas and Buttons enjoyed spending time together. He was a frequent visitor to her house, but he was never seen on the worktop again.

On his final day in the cul-de-sac, Douglas went on Guard Cat Duty with Buttons. From the window ledge in Diane and Jim's bedroom, together they supervised the milkman and then the woman who came to measure the living room of house number 4 as the humans there had ordered a new carpet.

Feeling rather peckish, the two cat pals went downstairs to Buttons' kitchen. Her leftover rabbit flavoured breakfast soon disappeared! Both animals sat contentedly on the rug in the living room and washed their whiskers.

Douglas then noticed something, something very intriguing. He put up a paw and swiped the strand of soft, blue wool which was just visible dangling over the sofa. To his astonishment, the ball of wool fell out of Diane's knitting bag and rolled onto the rug between the two feline friends. Buttons thought that Douglas was very clever to have found this interesting toy for them to play with.

They had a great game of pit-pat, passing the wool to each other, but the fun really started when the rest of the knitting fell down as well. One needle came out of the stitches looped on it and the jumper began to unravel. Buttons and Douglas leaped upon it joyfully. The wool seemed to wriggle as it unravelled and they had a marvellous time chasing it all around the room. Poor Diane was in for a nasty surprise when she came home later and saw that all her hard work had been undone.

After such a hectic morning, the two furry friends were in need of a snooze. Buttons jumped up onto the sofa and curled up contentedly, allowing Douglas the special privilege of sleeping in her Radiator Slouch Pouch. And before long, both cats were fast asleep. Wonderful!

Buttons Visits the Vet

Buttons Visits the Vet

Buttons, Jim & Diane at number 9

Chapter 1

Buttons was asleep. Fast asleep.

Suddenly she woke up with a start when the alarm clock went off. Diane yawned and switched off the annoying buzzer. Buttons jumped from her chair and onto the bed, just as she did most mornings. Usually, she landed expertly and exactly where she wanted, but not today. Today she only managed to get two of her four paws onto Diane's tummy – her front left paw and her back left paw. Her two other feet went down Diane's side so that Buttons fell into the small gap between Diane and Jim.

"Oops!" Diane exclaimed, climbing out of her side of the bed. "Come on then, Buttons, let's go and sort out your breakfast and put the kettle on."

Buttons would normally have been overjoyed to hear that as Operation Breakfast was her first important job of the day. However, she wasn't really feeling hungry yet, so she had a long stretch and contemplated just going back to sleep.

"Come on, Buttons!" Diane called.

Buttons decided to go downstairs after all. She jumped down off the bed but landed with a big wobble. What was up with the house today?

Buttons padded to the top of the stairs and went down the first couple of steps then stopped, confused. The stairs seemed to be moving! As Buttons tried to descend, the stairs swayed and she stumbled against the wall then bumped into the bannisters on the next step. She didn't understand what was happening, but Buttons was certain now that something was <u>Not Right</u>.

Diane called her again, so Buttons made her way slowly to the kitchen where Diane was putting her food dish on the floor.

"Look, it's duck today, your favourite," Diane encouraged.

Buttons gave the food an experimental lick, but it was no good. She didn't feel like eating at all, so she went to her cat flap to look outside for intruders into her garden. Buttons was horrified to discover that the outside world had gone all blurry and she couldn't really see out as she normally did. What was wrong with the world today?

Buttons decided to go outside and investigate, but the cat flap was being very naughty. When she tried to push her face against the flap to open it, the cat flap moved so that Buttons could not go through it. She tried three times in all, but the flap wouldn't cooperate. Poor Buttons didn't understand what was wrong, so she curled up on the doormat inside the back door instead.

Meanwhile, Diane had noticed that Buttons hadn't eaten any breakfast. This wasn't like Buttons at all! Diane watched in dismay as the little cat tried and failed to go through her cat flap. Diane forgot about making a cup of tea for herself and Jim, and rushed back upstairs.

"Jim!" she cried. "There's something wrong with Buttons!"

Jim had just finished getting dressed after his shower, so he went downstairs to see what the problem was. He found Buttons by the back door still. She didn't move when Jim called her and she didn't eat the piece of ham which he offered her from his sandwiches for lunch. Poor Buttons didn't even lift up her head to sniff the treat.

Jim was very worried. He bent down and looked carefully at Buttons. He noticed that her eyes were rather red and watery.

"If she is no better when we come home after work," he said to Diane, "we'll take Buttons to the vet."

Normally, Buttons would have run off in terror at the mere mention of the vet, but not today. Today she just sighed sadly.

Chapter 2

Buttons had a terrible day. She didn't do any of her usual jobs. Instead, she spent all day asleep and felt very sorry for herself when Diane and Jim came home. They noticed that Buttons hadn't eaten any food all day and she hadn't moved from her position by the back door. As they called her name and stroked her, Buttons opened her eyes. It was then that Jim and Diane could see that they looked worse than before. They were now very red and watery.

"Don't worry, Buttons," Diane soothed. "We'll take you to the vet and they will try to make you better."

Just as before, Buttons was too poorly to run away at the mention of the dreaded vet. She was so poorly that she didn't even try to escape when Jim picked her up and put her in her hated cat box.

"She is definitely very sick," Jim said. "I've never been able to get her in her box so easily before. She didn't even try to scratch me!"

Buttons lay in the cat box and looked balefully out at her humans, but she couldn't see them. Everything was too blurry and fuzzy. When it was her turn at the vets, Diane opened the cat box but Buttons was too ill to get out on her own. Jim lifted her out and carefully placed her on the examination table.

The vet did lots of tests on poor Buttons. He opened her mouth and peered inside. He looked in her ears and felt along her body with his gentle hands. He took her temperature, listened to her heart with his stethoscope, and then took a blood sample to be sent off to the lab. Finally, he lifted her left eyelid and held her eye open while he shone a little torch into it. He repeated this with her other eye.

Diane was so worried that she couldn't wait any longer. "What's wrong with her?" she asked. "Is Buttons going to be alright?"

The vet explained that he couldn't see the back of her eyes even with his torch because her eyes were all misty. Then he waved right in front of her eyes and finally he made a couple of sudden movements towards her face. Buttons didn't react at all.

"Now," said the vet gently, "try not to be worried. Buttons can't see at the moment so I want to keep her here in our pet hospital for a few days. We will do more tests and we can give her some medicine when we get the results. In the meantime, we will put special drops in her sore eyes, which will start to soothe them. We will do everything we can to make her better."

The nurse fetched a little bottle of special eye drops from the medicine cupboard. Then the vet held one eye open at a time while the nurse squeezed some of the soothing liquid into Buttons' eyes. Some of the eye drops ran down her face, but the nurse gently wiped her fur with some cotton wool.

"It's quite normal for the liquid to run like that," said the vet. "Don't fret as most of the medicine will have gone into Buttons' eyes."

Jim and Diane stroked Buttons and told her that they loved her, then the nurse carried her away to get her settled in a comfortable bed in the pet hospital.

"We will look after Buttons," the vet said kindly. "Give us a ring tomorrow morning and we will let you know how she is."

It was a very sad Jim and Diane who went home then. Their house seemed empty without their little cat and they both missed her dreadfully. It was very strange not to have Buttons jump onto their bed the next morning. Instead of Operation Breakfast for Buttons, Jim phoned the vets to ask how Buttons was.

"Buttons slept well for most of the night," explained the night nurse. "We will keep putting the special drops in her eyes every hour. Ring us again later and we will tell you if she is any better."

Chapter 3

Diane and Jim went off to work, but found it very hard to concentrate that day as they kept worrying about their little cat. However, they knew that her test results would soon be ready and then the vets would know the best medicine to help make Buttons better.

The day also passed rather slowly for Buttons in the pet hospital. She didn't like having the eye drops at first, but she soon got used to them and even came to enjoy the little strokes and kind words which always came from the nurses giving her the drops.

Returning home from work, the house still felt so empty without Buttons. However, there was good news when Jim phoned the vet: the test results were there and Buttons had already been given her first dose of medicine. The nurses continued with the eye drops and at last Buttons began to feel a little better and managed to eat a few tiny mouthfuls of cat food. Hooray for Buttons!

During the next couple of days, Buttons continued to have her medicine and eye drops. She felt a bit better every day and really relished the special attention of all the different nurses and various vets. When the vet next looked in her eyes, she was overjoyed when Buttons reacted to the light shining in from her torch.

"Buttons can see light now," the vet told Jim and Diane. "You will be able to take her home soon," she said.

Chapter 4

And so, it was a very happy Jim and Diane who took Buttons home after more than a week in the pet hospital. When Diane opened the cat box, Buttons jumped out and ran to her cupboard in the kitchen. She patted the cupboard door to remind her humans where her food was kept.

"Oh Buttons," laughed Diane and Jim, "you **are** better!"

When she had eaten some tasty cod flavoured cat food, Buttons went out through her cat flap. She had been very comfortable in the pet hospital, but it was so much better to be home again! Buttons was overjoyed to be back in her own garden and her humans came outside to play with her. They all had a wonderful time frolicking in the flowerbeds and gambolling on the lawn and under the tree.

While they all rested on the grass, Jim had a great idea.

"Let's have a party for Buttons to celebrate that she is well again. We can invite Granny and Aunty Paula," he announced.

"Oh yes," exclaimed Diane, "what a wonderful idea! And let's invite everyone in the cul-de-sac too. We can have cakes and tea and lemonade for all the humans and buy some treats for all the cats and dogs in our street too. Let's make it a fabulous garden party!" she added.

Diane and Jim were still planning the party as they made their way back indoors with the little black and white cat happily by their side.

After a little snack, Buttons jumped up onto the sofa. She was delighted to be home again and enjoyed all the lovely strokes from Diane and Jim. She spent a few minutes on Diane's lap then swapped over to sit on Jim's knees as well. Buttons settled her chin comfortably on her paws and drifted off to a wonderfully contented sleep.

Buttons Saves the Day

Buttons Saves the Day

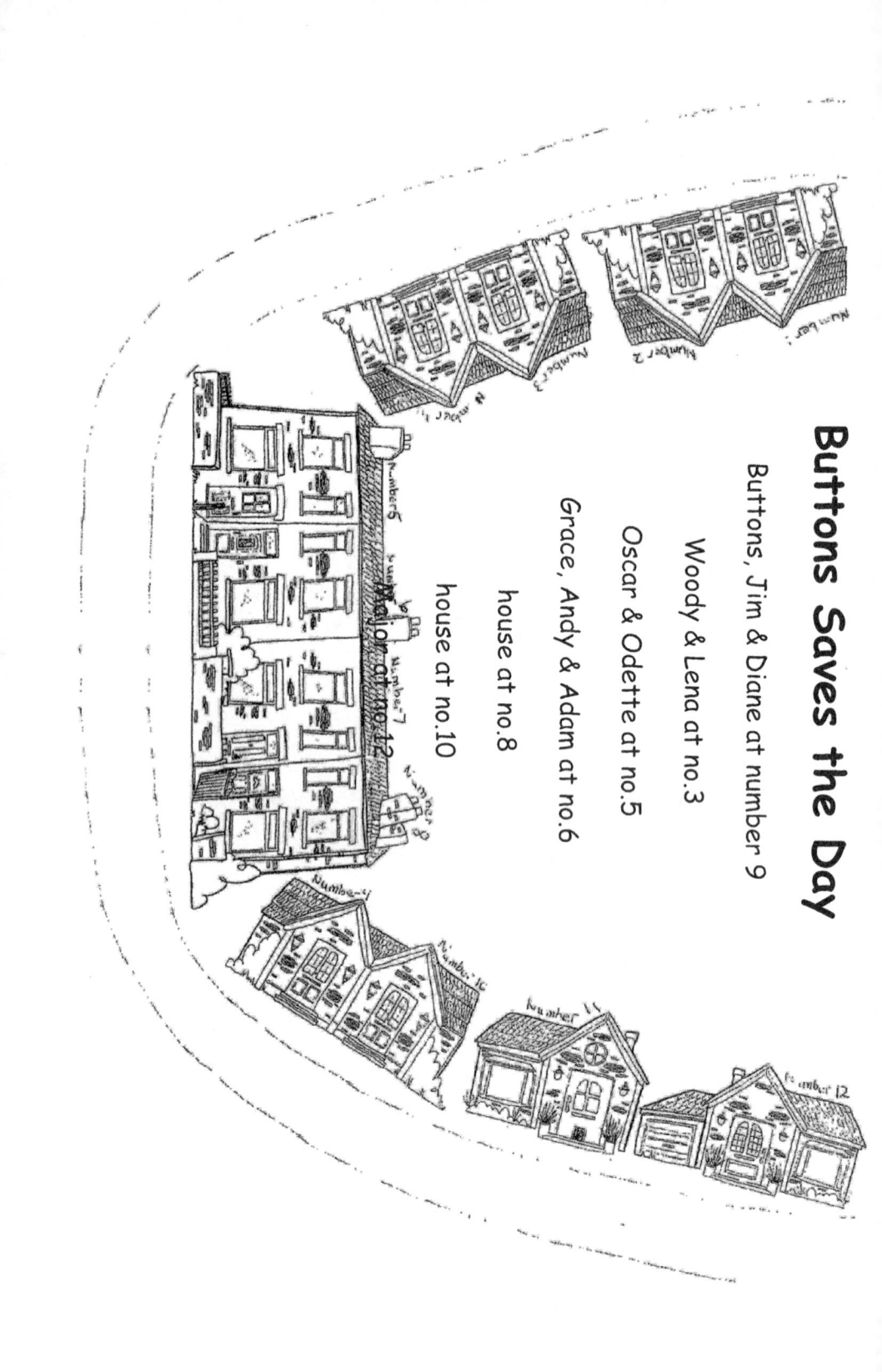

Buttons, Jim & Diane at number 9

Woody & Lena at no.3

Oscar & Odette at no.5

Grace, Andy & Adam at no.6

house at no.8

house at no.10

Chapter 1

Buttons was having a much-deserved snooze under the lilac bush in her back garden. As she slept, she had a tickling feeling in her tummy fur but she was able to ignore it. Cats need a lot of sleep.

Then she felt an itch on her back. She rolled over and tried to wriggle and stop the itch without being disturbed too much, but it was no good. The itching was terrible.

Buttons was wide awake now so she had a good long scratch all over. That felt better!

It was a Thursday afternoon in September. It had been a lovely day, one of those days that make you think that winter is a long way away. Buttons had enjoyed herself and spent most of her time relaxing in the sunshine, when she wasn't on Pussycat Patrol or Guard Cat Duty, of course.

Fully rested now, Buttons was just about to go indoors to see if any fresh food had somehow appeared in her bowl when she heard the engine of a strange van driving into the cul-de-sac. Like all cats, she was a curious creature so she had to investigate.

Wandering around to the front garden, she saw a woman unload something from her black van. Buttons didn't know what it was, so she watched to see what would happen next.

The woman put the strange thing on the grass outside the bungalow at number 12 and started it up. It made a loud buzzing sound and Buttons watched in wonder as the woman and her machine went all over the lawn. The little cat was amazed to see the grass getting shorter as they went. Buttons just *had* to inspect all the gardener's work as she made her way around the cul-de-sac.

But while the gardener and her lawnmower were cutting the grass outside Bob's house at number 8, Buttons leaped into the back of her black van and explored her interesting tools. She was particularly impressed with her garden fork which was so much bigger than the forks in Diane and Jim's kitchen!

Luckily, the gardener noticed the little Manx cat in her van when she packed away her equipment. Smiling, she picked Buttons up and put her on the pavement so she didn't drive away with an unexpected passenger.

Chapter 2

Buttons looked around, trying to decide on the cosiest spot for a snooze. Suddenly she heard a loud buzzing sound again. But how could this be right when the gardener had just driven away?

Determined to solve yet another mystery, Buttons climbed the tree in her back garden. From here she had a good view around much of the cul-de-sac, but she still couldn't locate the source of the noise. She listened very carefully and realised that it was coming from the other side of the fence at the bottom of her garden.

Buttons had never explored there before, but she bravely scrambled up the fence and jumped into the garden of the people who lived in the next road along from hers. The lawnmower lady was actually in the next-door garden, but Buttons didn't mind. She would have to explore this garden instead.

She found herself in a pretty back garden. There were colourful flowerbeds along one side and a pond right in the middle, surrounded by strange little figures. Buttons didn't know that these were garden gnomes, but she ignored them as she looked at the pond.

All of a sudden, she saw a flash of gold in the water and bounded over to see what it was. Fish! *Lots* of fish.

Entranced, she watched them swimming around, then heard a voice.

"Hello there," a man's kind voice said. "Who's an Ickle Pickle then?"

Buttons had no idea what this might mean, but she didn't have time to think about it. A woman darted out of the house and shouted at her!

"Go away, you nasty cat!" the woman cried. "You're not going to eat my fish. Shoo!"

"She's only looking at them," the man began.

But he got no further as poor Buttons dashed over to the fence and was over it in double-quick time. Safely landing back in her own garden, Buttons stood trembling in terror.

Chapter 3

Then she heard the welcome sound of Diane's car coming into the cul-de-sac. Fish, gnomes and strangers who shouted at her were instantly forgotten. Buttons ran to the front door. As Diane went inside, Buttons twirled her body around Diane's legs. While Diane was slipping off her sandals, the little Manx cat rubbed her head on Diane's ankles, purring loudly.

"I'm going as fast as I can," laughed Diane. "Please be careful, Buttons, or you will trip me up."

But Buttons didn't stop and trotted in and out of Diane's legs as they both made their way to the kitchen. Diane was glad to get there without falling over her pet and Buttons was glad to get her tea at last. Cats are not very patient animals.

That evening, Jim and Diane watched a film on the television. Buttons wasn't interested in it and so she curled up on Jim's lap for a nap. As soon as Diane went into the kitchen to put the kettle on, Buttons awoke immediately and rushed into the kitchen to show Diane where her food was kept. She patted her cupboard, mewling to get Diane's attention.

"Ok, Buttons, you can have a little sprinkle of your biscuits," Diane told her, putting a few salmon flavoured biscuits in her dish.

Buttons didn't thank Diane, of course. Nonetheless she was pleased with her snack.

Carrying two mugs of tea back to the living room, Diane found Jim scratching his legs.

"I'm all itchy!" he moaned.

"It's probably just a little heat rash," said Diane. "It has been quite warm today."

As her humans continued watching their film, Buttons made herself comfortable on Diane's lap and had another little snooze before going out through her cat flap for an extra Pussycat Patrol.

"Jim, I feel itchy too!" sighed Diane, scratching her legs.

"Oh dear. I think Buttons has got fleas!" Jim exclaimed. "Perhaps she has been snuggling up with a hedgehog again. I'll pop into the Vets after work tomorrow and buy some flea treatment for her and some flea spray for our carpets and furniture."

"And I will go to the supermarket and buy some fresh fish for her tea tomorrow. Hopefully that will distract Buttons while you put the treatment drops on her neck. She hated it last time. Poor Buttons." Diane said.

Chapter 4

The next day dawned warm and sunny again. Buttons was extra tired after a very restless night. She felt itchy all over and it was awful! She didn't know what was wrong, but she *did* know that she didn't like it.

Operation Breakfast went well and despite being so tired, little

Buttons was kept very busy that day. She watched all the comings and goings of everyone in the cul-de-sac, humans and animals alike.

She had a good game of Chase with Woody, her Dalmatian dog friend from house number 3, when he went out for a walk with Lena, his human.

She supervised the postman as he delivered the letters, noting that the twins, Odette and Oscar at house number 5, got lots of cards (it was their seventh birthday).

She was intrigued when a blue van appeared outside house number 10 next door, and a man got out and put up a ladder. Buttons remained on Guard Cat Duty as he climbed up and fixed a satellite dish to the chimney and connected it up with cables leading into the house. Then he collected up all his equipment and drove away.

At that very moment Buttons saw something moving in the grass. Cats are natural hunters and she chased it instinctively. The little creature ran away and escaped by squeezing itself right under the fence.

Buttons didn't hesitate. In an instant she had climbed the fence and leaped into the garden that backed onto her own. She was lightning-fast and successfully pounced on the other animal.

And there was the kind man with his cross wife.

"Shoo..." she began, but the man stopped her.

"What a clever cat!" he exclaimed. "Look what she has in her mouth."

"It's a r..." the woman began, but once again her husband stopped her.

"Remember, we don't say 'R-A-T' here!" he cried. "The clever Ickle Pickle has caught a 'Longtail' for us."

Buttons stood before them with the dead 'Longtail' dangling from her mouth.

"Well done!" they told her together.

"Thank you," the woman continued kindly, as Buttons dropped the creature at their feet and made her way back to her own garden. She felt very pleased with herself.

Satisfied that all was well, Buttons decided that a super long rest was in order. And so she was now happily curled up on the marvellous swing seat in Number 6's back garden.

Unknown to the human residents, Buttons often napped here. Grace, Andy and Adam had no animals of their own, so Buttons felt free to consider this garden as an extension of her own territory.

She was dozing happily when another van drove into the cul-de-sac. Dear Buttons just *had* to wake up and go to investigate. She noticed that it was not another black van nor another blue van, but a silver one this time. It parked outside the four terraced houses and a man and a woman got out. Both of them were wearing navy blue overalls and black caps. The woman locked the van and put the keys in her pocket.

Buttons didn't know who these two people were. They didn't have any ladders, or hoses, or lawnmowers, or parcels, or meter readers. Buttons wondered if *they* knew what they were there for, as the two newcomers spent quite a while looking around. Perhaps they were searching for something, she thought, as the pair wandered up and down the road. What were they doing?

Chapter 5

The woman rang the doorbell of the bungalow at number 12, while the man lurked around the side. However, they seemed to change their minds as Major started barking furiously.

Buttons was suspicious now and watched them approach her own house at number 9. Again, the woman rang the doorbell while the man went around the side of the house.

To Buttons' surprise, the man climbed in through the dining room window! Unfortunately, it had been left open as the weather was so warm. Once inside, the man opened the front door for his friend. Both humans started looking around the house. They opened a sack and began to put things inside it.

Buttons wasn't at all sure what was going on. Jim and Diane were still at work and neither Granny nor Aunty Paula were due to visit.

However, these strangers were in her house and it was nearly teatime. Buttons realised that she was very hungry indeed. She ran inside using her cat flap, but the two people ignored her as they were so busy putting valuables into their sack.

Obviously, they needed Teatime Training, Buttons thought. She approached the man as he was closest to her and weaved her body between his feet, miaowing to get his attention. She was very disappointed when he didn't move to the kitchen to feed her and went upstairs instead.

Buttons decided then to try and train the woman, so she rubbed her body on the woman's legs, twisting between them and mewling.

The woman fell over the feline hazard and landed awkwardly in a heap on the carpet. Buttons leaped safely out of the way, then jumped onto the woman's tummy. What a wonderful new game, she thought!

Just at that moment, Jim and Diane arrived home. They stepped into the living room and looked in horror at the woman lying on the floor. Buttons was on top of her and their valuables were tumbling out of the sack beside her.

"Quick," Diane said to Jim, "stand guard over this woman while I phone the police."

So, the female robber was caught red-handed with the loot she was trying to steal.

Meanwhile, the other thief was still upstairs. As soon as heard voices below him, he gave up searching for jewellery in the bedroom and sneaked down the stairs. Without being seen by Jim or Diane. He slipped outside to the silver van.

The police arrived as he was trying to force his way into the van. Unfortunately for him, the woman had the keys in her pocket. The policemen spotted his odd behaviour. One of the officers arrested him and put him in the back of their police car, while the second policeman went into house number 9 and arrested the woman thief. She was soon in handcuffs in the police car too.

As they were driven off to the police station, the robbers were both scratching madly at their legs and ankles. They had no valuables, but they did get little souvenirs of their failed robbery!

"Hooray for Buttons!" cried Diane and Jim. "What a clever cat!"

Buttons agreed, but there was only one thing on her mind now: Teatime. She ran to her cupboard, but Diane served up some fresh trout for her instead. Buttons was happily eating her little feast when Jim put the flea drops on the back of her neck. The liquid was cold and Buttons didn't like it at all. Fortunately, she was distracted as the fish was so tasty.

After their own meal of trout, which they enjoyed with mixed vegetables and rice, Jim and Diane sat in their garden with refreshing mugs of tea. Buttons came to join them and jumped up onto Jim's lap. They all relaxed in the evening sunshine.

What a day it had been!

Mollie's Manx Tails

The Buttons Prequel

Prologue Part 1

'**Manx cats**' are born without tails: sometimes they have a little stump of a tail but often have no tail at all. They are native to the Isle of Man but can now be found all around the world. They are particularly popular in America.

Anyone – human, cat or anything else - originating on the Isle of Man is '**Manx**', so our dear friend Mollie is Manx but she is not a '**Manx cat**' as she has a perfectly nice tail!

Manx folklore says that when Noah called them onto the Ark as the rains fell and the floods began to rise, the Manx cats did not come at once and only just managed to jump aboard as he was shutting the doors. Their tails got stuck in the doors and were left behind, so now true Manx cats are born without tails.

Prologue Part 2

Granny had a cat many years ago: a very friendly, boy cat called Sammy. He was ginger and stripy, with a white tummy and a mostly white face. One of his paws was white, as was one set of eyelashes with the others being ginger.

When little Mollie recently came into Granny's life, she jokingly referred to herself as 'Granny' because Sammy had been her pet so long ago. Of course, Granny knew that she wasn't *really* Mollie's granny – her real granny was a cat, naturally. But somehow Mollie and Granny suited each other and the name stuck.

And when something truly special happened, Granny thought of herself as a true Granny after all.

Chapter 1

Mollie felt odd, very odd indeed. She had no idea what the matter was, but she definitely knew that something strange was going on. She stretched out completely, from the tips of her black, triangular ears to the end of her furry, black tail. Her tummy felt lumpy and heavy, her head was pounding and even her little paws felt weird and sort of restless somehow.

She tried to smooth these feelings away with a good, long lick with her raspy tongue but it made no difference. She tried a mouthful of fresh food but even her favourite salmon-flavoured cat food didn't help. Sighing, Mollie pushed the bowl away and wondered what to do next.

Granny appeared then and smiled warmly at her little, black cat. Mollie loved Granny from the very roots of her black whiskers down, but today even Granny was behaving oddly. Granny showed her a cosy box, lined with folded towels and topped off with Mollie's favourite soft blanket. Mollie was puzzled – what was this strange box?

Then something even more peculiar happened. Granny bent down and lifted up the cat and placed her gently in the new box. She stroked Mollie and whispered warm words of encouragement, but Mollie didn't understand.

As soon as Granny stood up, Mollie jumped right out of the nest box. Puzzled, she watched as Granny moved her scratching post to the other side of the dining room and put the box neatly in its place. Granny patted the box and called to her, but Mollie wasn't going to be enticed into it. She turned her back on Granny and the box, swishing her tail widely.

"Come on, girl," Granny called softly, but this was the final straw for Mollie. With a final twitch of her whiskers, she made for her cat flap and escaped out into the sanctuary of the garden.

Chapter 2

Mollie stayed on high alert until she heard Granny's car starting up then driving away to the shops. Then the little cat curled up under her favourite bush and tried to go to sleep. This was usually very easily accomplished, but not today. Today the ground felt too hard, the leaves felt too prickly and the sun felt too hot even in the shade. Poor Mollie just couldn't get comfortable at all.

Later, Mollie heard Granny come back and then the unmistakable sounds of cupboards opening and shutting as Granny put away her shopping. Usually, the little cat would have dashed in through the cat flap to discover what treats Granny had bought for her, but not today. Even the sound of the fridge door with its promise of fresh fish couldn't tempt her.

Instead, Mollie set off for a lumbering stroll of the neighbourhood and refused to come in when Granny called her. Granny shook a new box of her favourite crunchy cat biscuits, but still Mollie took no notice. It wasn't until much later, when all the lights were off and the house was in its slumbering darkness that Mollie finally came in through the cat flap.

She sniffed at her bowl but really wasn't hungry. Normally, she would have enjoyed a tasty supper then headed up the stairs to curl up to sleep on the end of Granny's bed. But not today. Without knowing why, the little black cat wriggled her way to the very back of the storage area under the stairs. With her tummy heaving hugely, she squeezed herself into the very darkest corner and tried to get some sleep at last.

But sleep eluded our furry, black friend.

In the middle of the night, something most peculiar happened. Mollie had no time to wonder what on Earth was going on, when she seemed to encounter a second most peculiar event. And then it happened for a third and final time. Little Mollie was only just over a year old and hardly out of kittenhood herself. Absolutely nothing had prepared her for a night like this!

Chapter 3

Mollie's natural instincts had told her to hide and they were still in charge the next morning. The little cat heard Granny calling her and she listened as Granny cleaned out her bowl and filled it with fresh food. She kept perfectly still and quiet as Granny went around the house, looking for the cat and calling her name again and again. Granny even opened the front door and shook the biscuit box again, but her little pet didn't appear.

Puzzled and more than a little worried, Granny returned to the kitchen but no cat arrived through the cat flap.

Then Granny heard a sound. It was a tiny sound, the quietest squeak that you could possibly imagine. What was this noise? Was it a clue to Mollie's whereabouts?

Granny listened most carefully but couldn't work out where the noise had come from. She sighed and put her kettle on to boil for a welcome cup of tea. As it was brewing, Granny thought that she heard another tiny squeak. Determined to find out what it was and forgetting all about her cuppa, Granny searched high and low. Finally, she pushed the bead curtain to one side in the doorway to the storage area under the stairs and looked in. She saw a sight that was surprising and wonderful in equal measures.

Chapter 4

Yes, Mollie was there, her clear, yellow eyes peering back at Granny. At once Granny moved a box and her ironing board to clear a pathway to the furthest corner of the storage area. Granny smiled most warmly at the sight that greeted her: Mollie was there with three tiny bundles of fur!

Chapter 5

Granny sprang immediately into action. She reached for one tiny kitten, then gently patted it dry with a soft towel before placing it tenderly in the nest box she had ready. Twice more she collected the new-born kittens, dried them and put them safely in the box. Then her attention turned to the new feline mother.

Mollie was looking rather bedraggled. Her fur was also wet with the natural birth fluids and was standing up in strange tufts. She readily came to Granny but struggled away from the towel as Granny tried to dry her off. Instead, she padded over to her bowl and rapidly devoured first one, then two pouches of fresh cat food. Obviously, she was ravenous!

Granny stood by and watched as Mollie licked her whiskers clean after her welcome breakfast. What would her pet do now? She was still quite young herself and Granny feared that she might not accept her kittens or even know what to do with them.

But Granny need not have worried. Instinctively, Mollie ran to the nest box and jumped right in. She gave every kitten a quick lick then curled up on her side around her babies. Each tiny cat somehow also knew what to do and they instinctively searched for a teat and began suckling. Granny knew then that the new cat family would be fine. Smiling, she turned at last to her own breakfast.

Mollie did a great job of washing then feeding her kittens before the new feline family snuggled together for a good, long nap.

The kittens were indeed tiny and could easily have fitted into the palm of your hand! They were all three almost completely black but Granny was most surprised to find that only two kittens had tails like Mollie. The third kitten was a little Manx cat without even a stump of a tail. Obviously, either the kittens' father or Mollie herself had

Manx cat in their genes. Granny wasn't sure as Mollie was a rescue cat but it was certainly an interesting quirk of nature.

Chapter 6

The new-born kittens didn't move very far and were a few days old before they really started to move around the nest box. Their eyes were shut and they spent their time simply suckling their mother's milk or sleeping, all nestled together in a warm and cosy huddle. Mollie kept them clean and they were perfectly content.

Granny bought special cat food for Mollie with extra nutrition for mother cats. Because she was providing her babies with milk, Mollie naturally needed more nourishment than usual. She also enjoyed the cat biscuits specially prepared for mums and their kittens which were full of protein and particularly small, although it would be several weeks yet before any of the youngsters tried them.

Mollie spent most of her time in those first weeks in the nest box with her kittens. However, she still wanted to go outside now and then, always dashing back to her babies immediately if any of them so much as squeaked while she was away. Clearly, she never went far and stayed in range of hearing them if they needed her. As the kittens grew,

Mollie gradually left them for slightly longer and longer periods while they became increasingly independent.

Like most adult cats, Mollie recognised her name and would come if called – when it suited her, that is! Granny knew that the kittens would eventually find new and loving homes of their own, but of course she needed names for the babies now (their forever-families would choose their own names for them on adoption). But what should she call them?

For the first few days, all three youngsters looked very similar with silky, black fur like their mum. Of course, the Manx cat was a little more easily identified, but her sisters' tails were so minute that Granny couldn't really tell the baby cats apart in those early days. However, soon the little cats began to change, with one tailed baby in particular developing beautiful white patches over both her eyes. Well, the name for this kitten was obvious and she was thereafter known as Panda.

The Manx kitten developed a white front and white paws with a distinctive black spot on her right front paw. Granny thought she was as sweet as a peach so she was given the name Peaches. The third baby developed very slight brown, lengthwise stripes over her back but remained mostly black, so Granny named her Plum to match well with her sisters' names. Somehow, the alliteration of their names all beginning with 'P' was perfectly pleasing!

When the babies began running around, Granny laughed as she could so easily see the black spot on Peaches' paw because this feature was hidden when she was curled up, asleep. And when her sisters stood up, Granny smiled as they held their tiny tails upright, reminding her of meerkats!

Chapter 7

Books and the internet will inform you that kittens open their eyes from about three weeks old, but our little friends had their eyes open in just over two weeks.

It was also about then that they first began to try and escape from the nest box. Peaches was the bravest and most adventurous of the trio in just about everything, and was naturally first to climb over the side of the box. Mollie sprang immediately into action and lifted her back in, carefully holding in her mouth the skin and fur around the baby's neck. Undeterred, Peaches was soon out again and it wasn't long before Panda joined her. Plum was the smallest and shyest of the kittens but she also managed to climb out after another day or two.

To give the youngsters more space and the freedom to roam a bit, Granny constructed a "compound", as she laughingly called it. She used strong tape to join the edges of two planks of plywood with her sideboard and her dining room wall, thus creating a safe area in the corner of the dining room with the nest box and scratching post inside. She lined the whole area with old towels to protect the carpet from any little toilet accidents – they don't make nappies for kittens, do they? With the addition of their toy mice, tiny squirrel toy and their beloved ping pong balls, the compound was now complete.

The kittens seemed to love their new space and explored everything most thoroughly. Plum quickly took to curling up in the exact corner of the compound and her sisters sometimes joined her there. No-one spent much time in the nest box now and it wasn't long before Granny decided to take it away, leaving the folded blanket behind for sleeping on if anyone wanted it.

Chapter 8

A couple of days later, Granny was delighted to see Peaches sharpening her tiny claws on the scratching post for the very first time. Panda was the next to try it and they both seemed to love copying their mum in this. Plum waited another two days before she had a go too.

But a less welcome development came when Granny returned from visiting a friend and discovered only **two** kittens in the compound! Mollie was outside, lying in the sunshine by the front door. But which baby was missing and where was she?

Frantically, Granny searched the dining room and soon found an important clue: several books were jutting out from the bottom shelf of the bookcase. Pulling one out completely, Granny laughed to see little Plum, curled up quite contentedly in the furthest corner behind the other books. Granny wasn't at all sure how Plum had made her way there, but the answer came the next day – can you guess how the kitten had got behind the books?

Next morning, Granny was getting dressed after her shower when she heard the landline phone ringing downstairs. She grabbed her dressing gown and dashed downstairs to answer it. After chatting to her grown-up daughter, Diane, she returned upstairs and was amazed at the sight which greeted her: Mollie was there and she was carrying Panda in her mouth.

Granny had left one of her drawers open and was just in time to see Mollie jumping up into the drawer and placing poor Panda among her underwear!

Granny rescued the kitten and took her back downstairs to the compound, accompanied by a mewling Mollie. Just why the mother cat had tried to hide her baby, Granny didn't know. But she now suspected that Mollie had also been responsible for hiding Plum behind the books. What was Mollie up to?

Downstairs, Granny got her next surprise, for the books on the bottom shelf of the opposite bookcase were askew and one book had fallen out onto the carpet. Yes, I think you might have guessed the reason why: Plum was behind the books again! She was perfectly content but Granny decided to prevent this from happening again – what would happen if Mollie tried to hide a kitten behind the books on the top shelves?

Granny pushed all her books to the very back of the shelves and resolved to keep the door between the lounge and dining room shut from now on – not to keep the kittens from escaping, but rather to keep Mollie from hiding them all over the house!

Chapter 9

All three kittens were growing fast and soon began climbing the walls of the compound. Peaches was naturally the first to get right on top, using the folded edges of the towels for extra height. Granny watched as she bravely looked around then jumped confidently down. Granny smiled as Peaches scampered around the dining room, running under the table and chairs. However, when she returned to the outside of the compound, Peaches couldn't get back in so Granny gently lifted her over the wooden side.

It wasn't long before her sisters also managed to get out of the compound, even though Granny flattened the towels by the edges. Once cheeky Panda even climbed on top of her mother's head to gain extra height and Mollie gave her a little swipe of her paw in protest. Undaunted, Panda joyfully played hide and seek with Peaches under the legs of the furniture, joined eventually by Plum.

Escaping the compound was soon too easy for all three babies and they quickly learned how to jump up and get back in. Sometimes Granny found only Mollie to be inside, getting a few minutes of peace as her youngsters played chase through the dining room and on into the kitchen.

Chapter 10

As soon as the kittens began exploring the kitchen, Granny knew that she had to lock the cat flap – she simply couldn't risk any kittens copying Mollie and getting outside. They were far too tiny and could easily get lost or fall prey to a passing predator (it is recommended that kittens only go outside when they are over four months old, have been neutered and vaccinated and have human supervision at first).

Locking the cat flap also had another consequence: Granny had to get the litter tray ready for the cats to use as their toilet. She pushed the bead curtain to one side in the doorway to the storage area under the stairs, placed clean newspaper on the floor and put the tray on top filled with kitty litter – special pieces of absorbent material resembling small pebbles. Cats are actually very clean creatures, but the kittens would need to learn how to use the litter tray from their mum. Granny opened the back door for Mollie to go outside on her own whenever possible, though Granny couldn't always be there at the right time and Mollie would also have to use the "indoor toilet" when she needed it and couldn't get outside to her usual spots in the rough grass under the trees or hedge.

As the kittens grew and started exploring every nook and cranny of the dining room and kitchen, Granny also now abandoned the compound. She pulled off the strong tape from the edges of the two planks of plywood joined to her sideboard and dining room wall, feeling quite relieved that the wall and sideboard hadn't been damaged by the sticky tape.

However, she kept the area for the kittens, lining it with fresh towels and placing the scratching post in the corner surrounded by all their toys and ping pong balls.

The young cats enthusiastically explored the new kitten corner, immediately scattering the toys and ruffling up the towels. Granny's new job was now to straighten them all out whenever she passed by!

And now the kittens were more mobile, Granny let them into the lounge to give them more space to roam and explore. But she kept the door to the stairs shut for now to keep the youngsters safe.

The next morning, Granny came downstairs to find Mollie and Plum curled up together in kitten corner. Of Panda and Peaches, there was no sign!

As Mollie tucked into her breakfast and Plum jumped onto the lowest bookshelf for a nap, Granny searched high and low for the missing babies without success. Where were the two rascals?

Just then, the letterbox clattered so Granny went to fetch her post. Finding only a leaflet advertising a local pizza shop, she went to her recycling box on the shelf in the storage area under the stairs. Imagine Granny's surprise as two tiny pairs of eyes looked up at her and the leaflet she almost placed on top of the two furry faces!

And for some strange reason, the recycling box became a favourite sleeping place for all three kittens. Although they did snuggle up with Mollie on the sofa or in their kitten corner, the babies were more often found in the recycling box. For a long time after the kittens had left for their forever-homes, Granny couldn't help smiling at the memory of them whenever she put items in the recycling box.

Chapter 11

Granny's daughter Diane and her husband Jim came round to tea and to see the kittens.

"Come in," Granny said as Mollie wound herself around the ankles of their guests.

Jim stroked Mollie as Diane hung up their coats in the hall before they all went into the lounge. Granny left the newcomers there and busied herself in the kitchen with the kettle, tea things and biscuits, soon taking in the tray and placing it carefully on the coffee table.

"Where are the kittens, Mum?" asked Diane.

Although all four cats had so recently been together in the lounge, now there was only Mollie. The three humans searched the lounge, dining room and kitchen without finding the kittens. Even their beloved recycling box was empty.

Granny was really starting to worry, but Jim suggested that they drink their tea and the youngsters would soon reappear from their new hiding place. As they sat on the sofas, Diane suddenly laughed.

"Your cushion is purring!" she exclaimed, lifting up the cushion.

And yes, there were the three kittens, taking a catnap behind the cushion!

"Thank goodness we didn't sit down straight away and lean on them," said Granny.

From then on, the kittens were often to be found sleeping behind the cushions. Panda particularly preferred this new place although the recycling box was still a favourite with Plum and Peaches. Cats are experts at finding comfortable spots for a snooze, even if some of their selections are rather unusual.

As her sisters dozed, brave little Peaches jumped onto Diane's lap for a special stroke.

"Look, Jim, she's got a button!" Diane exclaimed, laughing.

And of course, she did. The black spot of fur on her otherwise white paws remained as she grew and grew, eventually being a quite distinctive feature of her right front paw when she was fully grown.

It was around this time that the kittens started playing chase around the sofas. Sometimes they ran their laps so fast that Granny couldn't tell who was in the lead! For a good few minutes, the little cats would run and run, then suddenly they all seemed to tire at the same time. Then they would collapse in a huddle on the carpet, almost instantly asleep. All cats spend a lot of time sleeping but feline babies sleep even more than adults. The average adult cat will snooze for about 15 hours a day, but this increases to around 20 hours daily for very young kittens and for elderly cats. In fact, it is thought that cats spend two thirds of their lives dozing and dreaming!

Chapter 12

Several days after Diane and Jim's visit, Granny came home and had another shock: all four cats were missing! She looked in kitten corner, but it was empty; there were only books on the shelves; the recycling box just contained some used envelopes and a flattened cereal box; a quick search behind the sofa cushions was unsuccessful too. Where were they all?

Puzzled, Granny sat on the nearest sofa and listened carefully. Yes, she could now hear the gentle sounds of cats purring but still she wasn't sure where they were. Inspiration suddenly struck and she peered **behind** her sofa. She smiled with relief as all four cats were revealed, sleeping in a cosy huddle in the tiny space between the sofa and the wall. There was just no accounting for all their choices of resting places!

The kittens were really growing fast and developing all the time. Some of these changes were more welcome than others! It was confident Peaches who first took a bite of Mollie's cat food. It was difficult to determine if she liked it or not, but soon her sisters also started tasting Mollie's food directly from her bowl. They were still suckling and Mollie's milk was definitely their main source of nourishment, but it was a clear sign that the youngsters were growing up.

The kittens were now much more active and loved exploring. Even Granny's handbag was regularly searched. Granny also had trouble keeping them downstairs and often had to rush after the little rascals who seemed determined to escape. And more than once Granny nearly tripped on a toy which had been abandoned in the middle of the carpet. The kittens' favourite ping pong balls were always vanishing, causing Granny to search for them in lots of odd places. She even had to bend right down and use a long ruler to retrieve those balls which had somehow found their way under the sofas.

Not so funny was the youngsters' new game of running up the curtains, leaving tiny holes in them from their little claws. One evening found Granny gently removing Plum from the lounge curtain only to see Panda swinging from the cable of the landline phone. Peaches also loved climbing and swinging on the bead curtain separating the kitchen and the storage area under the stairs. After the kittens had moved to their forever-homes, it took Granny a long time to untangle the beads.

Mollie was developing too. Gradually, she spent longer and longer outside on her own, knowing instinctively that her babies were becoming more independent. And Granny felt that a significant step came one day when she was stroking Plum on her lap. Mollie jumped onto the sofa, swiped poor Plum off Granny's knees and took her place!

All these developments are quite natural and are found in the wild with bigger cats such as tigers, leopards and cheetahs. In the wild, the mums will eventually leave their youngsters to make their own ways in the world (but not lions who live in groups called <u>prides</u>). Granny knew that this time had arrived when she came home one day to find Mollie hiding alone behind the smallest sofa. She began meowing most piteously as her babies jumped on her and ran right over her as they played chase around the sofas.

Mollie and her beautiful kittens were clearly ready to move on to the next stages of their lives.

Epilogue Part 1

Granny shed more than a tear or two on the day that the kittens departed for their new homes. But she knew that each kitten would be well looked after in their new families and she smiled as she thought that the three beautiful bundles of fur would bring much joy and share much love in their forever-homes.

Goodbye and good luck, you three gorgeous girls!

And Mollie? Well, she was delighted to be able to sit comfortably on Granny's lap with no-one pulling her tail or jumping on her! She stretched out contentedly on her favourite cushion and relished the peace and quiet which reigned once more in Granny's house.

Epilogue Part 2

Panda was adopted by a happy family who lived in the south of the Isle of Man. She enjoyed all the attention of being the only cat in the household and was loved by everyone. The white patches over her eyes remained as very striking features, and her new family still call her Panda.

But she was the only kitten to keep her original name. Plum is now called Hiccup and she has a wonderful life with the elderly couple who adopted her. They all live together in a quiet street in Douglas, the capital of the island.

And do you know what became of the Manx cat, Peaches? Well, she now lives at number 9 in a quiet cul-de-sac in the west of the Isle of Man. Her humans are called Jim and Diane and she is now called Buttons – but that is quite another story!

<u>The End of the Stories. Read on for the Quizzes</u>

Quizzes

<u>Buttons – suggestions for your own illustrations</u>

<u>Hello Buttons!</u>

Buttons leaving her purple paw prints on Joe's painting.

<u>Buttons in Trouble!</u>

Buttons scattering leaves with Woody, her Dalmatian dog friend.

Plus, Buttons jumping joyfully into the cornflakes which Granny spread in the kitchen.

<u>Buttons on Holiday</u>

Any of the yoga poses/balances with Buttons 'helping'!

<u>Christmas Buttons</u>

Buttons and Jim with one end each of the tinsel.

Plus, Buttons with Dolly and her kittens.

<u>Buttons in Love!</u>

Buttons and Douglas playing joyfully with the wool and knitting.

Easter Buttons

Buttons patting the 'toy' chick, perhaps with Easter eggs in colourful, shiny wrappers in the background.

Plus, Buttons being rescued from the tree by the fireman.

Buttons and the TT

Buttons standing on top of Stephen's motorbike.

Buttons has a Plan

Smoky asleep in her fleecy, pink Slouch Pouch and Buttons using one of her toys to wake him.

Buttons Visits the Vet

Buttons on the examination table at the vets.

Plus, party scene to celebrate that Buttons is well again.

Buttons Saves the Day

Buttons admiring the fish in the fish pond.

Plus, the robbers itching terribly.

What other ideas do you have?

And how about drawing some pictures to illustrate 'Mollie's Manx Tails'?

*Did you notice the word play with **tails** and **tales**?

Words which sound the same but mean different things are called **homonyms** or **homophones**. Can you think of any other examples?

Buttons Quiz Question

Buttons lives with Jim and Diane at Number 9 in a quiet cul-de-sac on the beautiful Isle of Man.

Look carefully at this little picture of their house – is it a view of the front or the back? Perhaps you could compare it with the view of the cul-de-sac at the front of this story.

177

Clues

1. Where would the lanterns most likely be?
2. Would the letterbox be at the front or the back?
3. Where would you put the cat flap? You can look in the story to check – were you right?

The End of the Quizzes

The Complete Buttons Collection

Have you ever wondered what cats do all day?

Meet Buttons, a little black and white Manx cat who lives in a quiet cul-de-sac on the beautiful Isle of Man. Join this friendly cat on her adventures and find out what she gets up to – you may be surprised!

Children of all ages will love this new Collection of hilarious stories starring the friendly little Manx cat – and will never look at a cat the same way again!

This Collection also features <u>Mollie's Manx Tails</u>, the purr-fect prequel to the Buttons stories. This fictionalised, true tale follows Mollie as she becomes a new feline mum. Find out what happens as her three kittens grow and develop before eventually moving on to their forever-homes. Discover which kitten will be re-named 'Buttons' and learn some fascinating facts along the way.

<u>You may also enjoy</u>: CB (a very special cat with a secret double life), Creative Creatures, Snazzle Dazzle, Six Special Agents, The Really Wild Wildlife Park, Daisy's

Days Out, The Whimsical Collection, Fairytales: The New Collection,

The Wallababies and The Fairy Bridge Fairies.

Printed in Great Britain
by Amazon